WHAT PEOPI
TARA L. COLE AND EVERYDAY PRAYERS FOR
THE SCHOOL YEAR...

Few things are more terrifying for a mom than sending their child to school. Equivalent to the great unknown, we often feel like we're tossing them to the lions, knowing they'll return with scrapes, bruises, and wounds deeper than stitches could ever heal. More than anything, we want to protect them from influences, ideas, and words that have the potential to derail them and leave them floundering. I can think of no better protection for our children than our prayers as moms. In this practical book, Tara equips and trains us to be powerfully protective parents as she daily leads us through key prayer points that invite the Godhead into every aspect of our children's lives. Full of Scripture, each day includes practical steps on how to partner with God and trust Him for the security and protection that only He can bring.

—*Kim Wahl*
Pastor and author, *The Complaining Cure*

I can't think of anything that stirs up more excitement and fear simultaneously in the hearts of parents and kids alike than the start of a new school year. The truth is we can't always be with our kids, but our prayers can. I'm so grateful to have Tara to guide us through the process of praying with and for our kids. Her prayers are engaging and encouraging; they remind us that we get to partner with a great big God in the lives of our kids. You will return to *Everyday Prayers for the School Year* over and over through the years and have a beautiful record of God's faithfulness in the process. These prayers will be a springboard for your own prayers as you talk to the Father about the things that matter most.

—*Stacey Thacker*
Author, *Threadbare Prayer*

Tara Cole has written a thoughtful, encouraging, and very practical guide for every mom who wants to intentionally pray for her kids. However, you'll likely find you'll grow just as much as your kids as you are consistently and gently pointed back to God and His incredible promises.

—Christie Thomas
Author, *Fruit Full: 100 Family Experiences for Growing in the Fruit of the Spirit*

Tara Cole is a gifted writer with a knack for crafting words that pour blessings into a mama's heart. *Everyday Prayers for the School Year* is the perfect resource moms need to help their children flourish both in and out of the classroom. Packed with personal stories, biblical truth, and amazing prayer prompts, Tara ties it all together each day through practical life application. There's a plethora of quotes we can glean from like, "When we suffer or are put under pressure, it teaches us endurance." So good! I love that these words come straight from the heart of both a mom and a teacher who is relatable and abides in Jesus. In every turn of the page, there's encouragement, grace, and lifelong lessons we can all learn from on both the good days and the hard days. I cannot recommend this book enough, and it will surely become a mainstay for this school year and all the school years to come.

—Doris Swift
Author, speaker, and host, *Fierce Calling Podcast*

Sending our kids to school can be scary, but *Everyday Prayers for the School Year* reminds us that God is always with our children (and with us). Each day shares a story, Scripture, and something extra to think about—and feels kind of like sitting down with the author for a cup of coffee. Warm and reassuring, this book should be on every mom's school supply list.

—Mary Carver
Author, *Prayers from the Parking Lot*
Host, *The Couch Podcast*

As a busy mom and former military spouse, I have spent a good portion of my parenting years solo, and I have learned that while I may be parenting without my spouse, I can't parent on my own. I need strength and guidance from the Lord, as well as the support and exhortation of friends and fellow moms. This is exactly what Tara does in *Everyday Prayers for the School Year*. She comes alongside moms as a friend, encouraging us while pointing us back to the One who loves our kids more than we could ever imagine. Through this thirty-day devotional, Tara leads us through a quick devotional, prayer, Scripture, and reflective questions. It's the perfect way to start each day during the school year or any other time of year.

—*Alana Dawson*

Podcast editor, producer, and coach

Host, *The Podcasting Party*

DEDICATION

To Ethan, Liam, and Luke.
These prayers were first prayed over you
before this book was even a glimmer of a thought.

EVERYDAY PRAYERS
PRAYERS
— FOR THE —
SCHOOL
YEAR

A 30-Day Devotional & Reflective Journal for Moms

TARA L. COLE

WHITAKER
HOUSE

Everyday Prayers for the School Year
A 30-Day Devotional & Reflective Journal for Moms

taralcole.com
www.facebook.com/overacup
www.millionprayingmoms.com

ISBN: 978-1-64123-844-1
eBook ISBN: 978-1-64123-845-8
Printed in the United States of America
© 2022 by Tara L. Cole

Whitaker House
1030 Hunt Valley Circle
New Kensington, PA 15068
www.whitakerhouse.com

Library of Congress Cataloging-in-Publication Data (Pending)

1 2 3 4 5 6 7 8 9 10 11 ᴜᴊ 29 28 27 26 25 24 23 22

CONTENTS

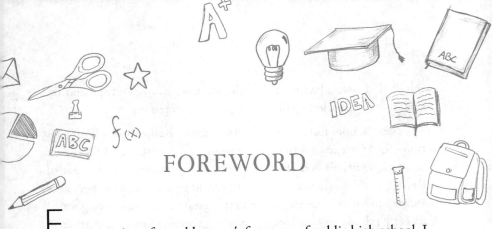

FOREWORD

Every morning of my oldest son's first year of public high school, I dropped him off, drove home, walked into his room, and laid on his bed, begging God to cover him and keep him safe.

You see, we had just transitioned him from a couple of years at a small, private, Christian school, and before that, he'd been homeschooled his whole life. He was encountering things that year that we had never experienced before as a family, and I'm not sure any of us knew what to do with them.

Looking back, I know that much of what we dealt with was simply growing pains—for him and for us. As we were trying to help him take it all in and interpret his experiences through the lens of God's Word, we were doing the same thing with our own experiences. It challenged us to get outside of our box and look at the world in different ways. I'm grateful we've had the experience of participating in almost every kind of educational option available to us over the years, but it was a hard season, and we struggled as God asked us to expand and learn new things.

Every family goes through difficult times. I know many parents who have taken an opposite path to ours, transitioning from public school to homeschool, and still encountered struggles and spiritual opposition. The enemy *will* throw things at our children—at us—in an effort to fulfill his plan to steal, kill, and destroy. (See John 10:10.) It doesn't matter how our children are educated; the world will find them.

I was a child of the 1990s, and while I faced my fair share of bullies, temptations, and fears, I did not experience the world the same way my children do today. If I had a bad day at school, home was my refuge. If I needed a break, I could get away from everyone and feel safe in the warm, loving home my parents offered me.

Now, school follows our children home. Bullies spread information—or worse, pictures—of our children's mistakes and most awkward moments all over the world before we even know it's happened. Recent statistics show that our children, at younger and younger ages, are dealing with depression, anxiety, and even suicidal thoughts, all directly related to the device they can't seem to function without—their phone. Maybe, if we dig down to the heart level, our kids are experiencing the same challenges we did, but I think we can all admit that the expression of those challenges is entirely different. So many parents find themselves asking the question, "How in the world do I do this?"

So, what is a God-fearing, normal Christian parent to do? How can we protect our children from everything the world throws their way?

We pray.

I know that may seem like a simple or even trite response to some pretty loaded, very serious questions. I want to assure you, at the time I'm writing this, I'm still raising two teenage boys who are in the thick of it. While we waited longer than most parents to allow our children to have phones and even social media at all, they do have them now. I know what you're going through! We do our very best to shepherd our boys and believe that God's Word applies even to the way we handle cell phone usage and the latest social media app. But it isn't easy. Nothing about parenting today is easy, but God has given us a way to partner with Him in the parenting of our children, no matter what period of history we live in. As believers, through prayer, we have direct access to the King of Kings and Lord of Lords, the Creator of our children's hearts, and the One who breathes life into their bodies.

I don't know exactly how prayer works, but I believe it does work because the Bible says it does. Somehow, God uses our prayers for our children as a part of what He's accomplishing in and through them, for their good and His own glory.

Parenting can leave us feeling helpless. Prayer fills us with holy purpose. That's why my dear friend, Tara Cole, has written this beautiful prayer journal for parents of school-aged children—to fill you with holy purpose and the knowledge that you are not helpless. Prayer is not passive. It's a preemptive, strategic partnership with God. Tara understands the needs of moms today and knows how to fight for them in prayer. She's a faithful praying mom, and I can't think of a better person to lead us on this journey.

It's my fervent hope that as you spend the next thirty days with Tara in prayer for your school-aged children, God will meet you with the knowledge that prayer—simply talking to Him, asking for His wisdom—is *not* a last resort. It's your proactive privilege as a child of the King, and it's the first and best response to the challenges of parenting.

It's also my prayer that you will fall in love with the method we use of praying God's Word back to Him. At Million Praying Moms, we believe there's no real wrong way to pray. But when you pray God's Word—seeking not to take it out of context or use it for something other than what God intended—you can never go wrong. It has the power to divide and change hearts (see Hebrews 4:12) and always accomplishes exactly what God purposes for it (see Isaiah 55:11).

Together,
Brooke McGlothlin
Founder, Million Praying Moms

ACKNOWLEDGMENTS

Thanks be to God first for doing a lot with my little. I did my best to show up faithfully where He led, even when it seemed to be the wrong direction. He has been faithful and has already done *"far more abundantly"* with this prayer journal than I could *"ask or think"* (Ephesians 3:20). I can't wait to see what You do next!

Thank you to my husband Jeremy, who has been my emotional and tech support for over twenty years. I could not do what I do without you, babe. To my boys, who encourage me and put up with being my guinea pigs for every crazy idea I have. My prayer is always that you love God first and most. Hopefully, some of those ideas help.

Thank you to the Whitaker House team, especially Christine and Peg. You've made this publishing journey a joy. Thank you!

Thank you to my text pray partners Sherri, Mandy, Crystal, Kara, Kara, Jacqueline, Julie, and Terri. Your prayers and friendship have meant the world to me. Doris Swift and Christie Thomas, my writing buddies, your encouragement and advice mean more than I can say. Thank you to my beta readers and Patreon partners Matt, Kara, Shonda, Shanna, Sarah, Amy, Melody, Angela, and Miriam. Your feedback and encouragement have helped to shape this book. To the Breakfast Club, your prayers mean so much. Thank you to my podcast coach, Alana Dawson, and my writing coaches, Brooke McGlothlin and Stacey Thacker. You are all more than coaches; you're my friends, and I could not have done this without you. Brooke, thank you for giving me the opportunity to write this book. It has become so much more than either of us could have imagined!

Thank you to all of you! It truly takes a village, and you are mine.

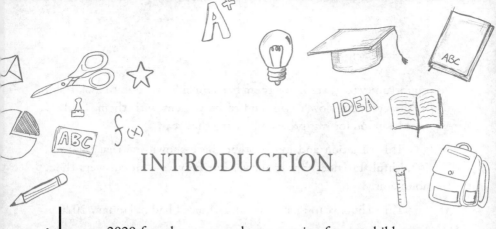

INTRODUCTION

January 2020 found me on my knees praying for my children—again.

Even though I'm a teacher, my university has classes year-round. The past few summers, I had enrolled my boys in a childcare program, but it was no longer a good fit, and they were begging me to not put them there again. I didn't have any clear options and dreaded what the summer would hold.

For weeks, I scrambled to find a good solution. I researched other options, stressed over my schedule, and prayed for ideas. My first thought each morning was what our summer would look like. It was the main topic of all my conversations, and I'm sure my husband and friends grew tired of my fear-filled talk.

For eight weeks, I carried around the burden and guilt of not being able to be there for my kids like I wanted to be.

Finally, right before spring break, a good friend said she could watch my children. I felt relief knowing they would have fun and be with friends, but I still wanted to be with them myself.

You know where this is going, right?

COVID-19.

My schedule and theirs was utterly wiped clean and completely rearranged when the pandemic hit the United States in March 2020. That spring, we *all* did school from home. That summer, we had months together, day in and day out.

While being home with three kids was exhausting, I am so grateful for that time I had with them. I was delighted to have the opportunity to get to know them better inside and out, to look them in the eyes and slow down, and to be present with them. Daily, I thanked God for His provision during that year.

This situation and many others have shown me that my God is faithful. He doesn't just answer our prayers—He answers them abundantly.

This school year, I have the same choice I had in January 2020.

I can choose to worry and stress over my sons' school situations, to carry that burden of uncertainty and frustration. Or I can choose to focus my eyes on Jesus and to trust Him.

Today, I'm choosing trust.

Here is a verse that has encouraged me often as I face the unknowns related to raising kids: "*We do not know what to do, but our eyes are on you*" (2 Chronicles 20:12).

This is my prayer for us as we all go through this school year. Actually, it's the perfect verse to pray any time because our children will always face challenges and uncertainties. It's tempting to dread those challenges. It's tempting to stress over what school will or should look like. It's tempting to fear circumstances that can impact our children for years to come.

But as I look at the Bible and my own life, I'm reminded over and over again that even when times are uncertain, I can look to the One who has all the answers. He might not reveal them to me yet, but He has them, and I can trust Him with my children's future.

No matter what choice you've made to educate your children—public school, online, distance learning, or homeschool—as mothers, we have similar concerns and prayers for our children, prayers about our children making friends, connecting to teachers, learning in class, and growing in their gifts and character. As we consider this school year, we can choose to be anxious or choose to trust.

Let's choose trust together.

FRIENDS

Friendships are at the forefront of many conversations around my table. No matter your schooling choice, we all hope our kids will make good friends who point them to Jesus, and they will be those friends for others. Some kids are gifted in this area and can make friends with anyone, while others struggle for years, and it breaks our mama hearts to watch that struggle.

We know the importance of good friends and hear over and over that the difference maker in many young adult lives has been their friends.

This school year, we're going to cover our children's friendships in prayer and ask God to do what only He can.

TEACHERS

Whether your children are in a classroom face-to-face, distance learning, or homeschooling, we all want teachers for our kids who don't just teach them reading, writing, and arithmetic but really see and hear our children and value them for who they are.

One of my boys is a strong leader. In our karate classes, I can easily tell the type of instructor by the way that son acts. Teachers who understand him and require him to do his best get that boy to follow along and listen through a forty-five-minute class. Teachers who treat him like a cute little kid are going to have a terror on their hands. He lives up to their expectations and takes the whole class with him.

For him and my other sons, I constantly pray that their teachers will have insight into what they need and love them for who they are.

In our prayers in this journal, we'll join together and pray for our children's teachers, whoever they may be, asking God to grant them wisdom and insight this school year.

CLASSES

We send our kids to school or teach them at home in the hopes they will get a good foundation in the basics so they can do well in other pursuits, but sometimes they still struggle. They feel defeated by work that is hard or instructions they don't understand. Getting them motivated can feel like pushing a boulder up a hill of slime.

Whether the basics come easily or are a constant struggle, our prayers in this journal will focus on God granting them understanding, a good work ethic, and endurance when things get hard.

GIFTS

More than the basics, it's our hope as mamas that those God-given gifts we see in our children will grow and flourish. Yes, I want my kids to do well in writing (I'm an English teacher after all!), but more than an A on a report card, my constant prayer is that I partner with God to help grow and develop my children's gifts.

I have one son who does well in school, but his real gifts lie in relationship building. He is the most generous boy you have ever met. Recently, he willingly let his brother borrow a brand new scooter for several rides up and down our street. When his friends come over, he's the one who thinks to get drinks and snacks before they even ask.

As I think about his gift, my prayer is that I can help him use it wisely but that others don't take advantage of him and harden his heart. I pray he makes it to adulthood just as generous and thoughtful as he is now.

My other sons are similar. They have gifts that don't fit the mold, and I love them so much for it! This school year, I want them to grow in those gifts and learn how to serve God through them. He has a purpose for them. My job is to steward them well.

CHARACTER

Beyond their gifts, we all hope that our children will be men and women of character. We pray that God will grow in them the fruits of the Spirit—love, joy, peace, patience, kindness, goodness, faithfulness, gentleness, and self-control. It can be tempting to try to force the development of these traits in us and our children, but it is really the Spirit who grows them in us all.

In our final prayers of this journal, we'll focus on the fruits of the Spirit and asking God to grow them in our children's lives. Because even as important as reading, writing, and arithmetic are, *who* our children are becoming is even more important.

With all the choices we have to make, school years can seem scary, full of dread and uncertainty, but with our focus on Jesus, we can have hope. We can lift our eyes up from the circumstances surrounding us and our children and place them firmly on the One who is in control. As we seek Him this school year, He can turn our dread into delight, our stress into song, and our fear into a focus on Him.

As a special gift for you, I've designed a bookmark with a reminder for each of the thirty days of prayer in this book. Find it and other school prayer resources at taralcole.com.

Grace and peace,
Tara L. Cole

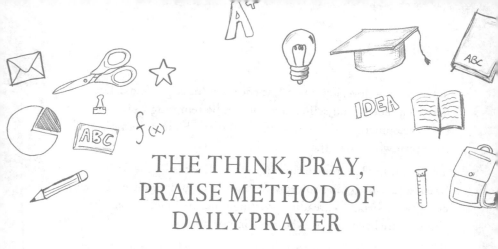

THE THINK, PRAY, PRAISE METHOD OF DAILY PRAYER

Brooke McGlothlin
Cofounder, Million Praying Moms

When I first started praying for my own children, I was inspired by two important truths about God's Word:

1. *The word of God is living and active, sharper than any two-edged sword, piercing to the division of soul and of spirit, of joints and of marrow, and discerning the thoughts and intentions of the heart.* (Hebrews 4:12)

2. God declares, *"My word that goes out from my mouth...will not return to me empty, but will accomplish what I desire and achieve the purpose for which I sent it"* (Isaiah 55:11 NIV)

If those two verses were true—and I believed they were—then it seemed to me that there could be no better thing to pray than God's Word itself! Because this experience was so deeply profound for me, it's the same one I've used to teach other women to pray. I call it my "Think, Pray, Praise" method. It isn't really rocket science, just a practical, biblical way to pray the Word of God over yourself or the people you love. It's also the method we use in Million Praying Moms' Everyday Prayers journal library. Let me walk you through it step by step.

THINK

On each daily page, we give you a verse to pray to make it easy for you to follow this prayer method. However, you can always search the Scriptures for yourself to find a verse you'd like to pray instead. After you've chosen it, reflect on, process, and meditate over your verse. If you have time, read a few verses that come before and after your verse, or even the entire chapter of the Bible so you can have the proper context from which to understand it. Consider what God is speaking to your heart through His Word and through this verse. Dream about the future and what it might look like to see the message of this verse come to fruition in your life, or in your children's lives. In a small way, analyze the verse and figure out what you're inspired to pray.

PRAY

For almost ten years, my desire has been to allow my prayers to be inspired by God's Word. I try very hard not to take verses out of context, or use them for a purpose or meaning other than that which God intended for them. Reading the verse in context, as I just suggested, really helps with this. Once I've selected a verse, I craft it into a prayer. I usually stay as word-for-word as I can and then pray that verse back to God. You can see an example of a "Verse of the Day" and the prayer we craft from it for you on the daily pages of this journal.

Once you have your verse and prayer, use your thoughts about them as a jumping-off point to allow God's Word to move you and shape your prayers.

PRAISE

Praise is my favorite part of this method of prayer! Praising God is like putting on a pair of rose-colored glasses; it literally changes the way you see the world around you.

New York Times bestselling author Ann Voskamp writes:

The brave who focus on all things good and all things beautiful and all things true, even in the small, who give thanks for it and discover joy even in the here and now, they are the change agents who bring the fullest light to all the world. Being joyful isn't what makes you grateful. Being grateful is what makes you joyful.[1]

When we pause to deliberately reflect on the good things God is doing in our lives right now, it changes everything. (This can be even the tiniest of things we have to look hard to see, like having to clean for a Bible study group in your home. You might not want to clean, but at least you have people coming over to discuss the Word of God with you!) Instead of focusing on all we don't have or don't like (such as cleaning), gratitude for what we do have (being with brothers and sisters in Christ) blossoms in our hearts, truly making us joyful. Each day, I try to write down just a few things I'm grateful for, praising God for His continuous work of grace in my life.

BONUS

You might notice the lines for a to-do list on the daily pages. I love that little block because I find that when I sit down to pray, my mind gets flooded by all the things I need to do that day. Every. Single. Time. I feel the urgency of my schedule begin to take over, distracting me from the time I so desperately need in God's Word and prayer. Taking a minute to jot down my to-do list before I get started is kind of like doing a brain dump each day. If my list is written down, I won't forget what I have to do that day. This frees me up to spend the time I've allocated in prayer without worry stealing it from me.

PRAYER REQUESTS

Part of being a woman of prayer is interceding on behalf of others. My life literally changed the day a good friend held my hands in hers and said, "Let's pray about this now" instead of telling me, "I'll pray for you." You won't always be able to pray for others in person, but keeping track of their needs on a prayer list like the one at the

---

1. Ann Voskamp, *One Thousand Gifts: A Dare to Live Fully Right Where You Are* (Nashville, TN: W Publishing Group, 2010).

bottom left of the daily pages is a great way to make sure you're being faithful to cover them in prayer.

GO!

I am so excited about the journey of prayer you hold in your hands. Each day begins with a devotion written specifically for you, and concludes with extra verses and questions for reflection that are a perfect way to take your study of joy to the next level or use with a group. We now consider you part of our Million Praying Moms family!

Connect with us at www.millionprayingmoms.com and keep us posted about the things God is doing in your life as you pray.

DAY 1

MAY THEY KNOW
GOD IS WITH THEM

READ ROMANS 8

*What then shall we say to these things? If God is for us,
who can be against us?*
—Romans 8:31

My cell phone rang as I left my last class of the day on a Tuesday afternoon.

"Hello, Mrs. Cole? This is the principal from your son's school. He was in music class, and another student jumped on him and choked him. He's okay, but he went to the nurse's office…"

As I hung up the phone, I was furious. This wasn't the first time I'd been called about my son being attacked by this student, but I was determined it would be the last.

Thankfully, based on my mom's sound advice, I didn't go full mother bear that afternoon, but I did pray and talk to friends who worked in the public school system.

The advice was not encouraging.

Due to the circumstances surrounding the situation, it did not look good. My friends were certain that, at the very least, my son would have to switch classes. But I didn't want that because he was excelling with his current teacher.

So, I prayed.

Armed with documentation of the previous incidents, I was ready to talk to the school officials, but God's Spirit said, "Wait." Although I didn't understand why I should wait, on Wednesday, I waited and prayed.

On Thursday, I emailed the principal to request a meeting. Instead, she called me, and I calmly explained the relationship and struggle between the two boys over the last year and a half.

I wanted to rant, I wanted to...but God.

She listened, and then told me she would see what she could do.

Later that day, she called back. "The other student will be moved to another class tomorrow."

My friends were in shock! The only explanation I have is "but God."

I still don't know what God did or how His Spirit moved on Wednesday while I waited, but I am confident He moved in the waiting.

Waiting is hard. Trusting is hard.

As moms, we know all too well that God doesn't promise an easy road for us or our kids. As much as we'd love to protect them from heartaches, it just isn't possible. Jesus even tells us in John 16:33 that we will have trouble, but we can still be confident because He has overcome the world.

Then, in Psalm 46:1–2, we're reminded:

God is our refuge and strength, a very present help in trouble. Therefore we will not fear though the earth gives way, though the mountains be moved into the heart of the sea.

God doesn't tell us the earthquake isn't scary. He doesn't say that moving and shaking mountains aren't dangerous. However, He does say that we can release any fear because He is our refuge and strength, and He is with us.

This idea is shown clearly in one of my favorite Bible stories in 2 Chronicles 20. During the reign of Jehoshaphat, who became king of Judah after his father Asa died, three large armies came to attack Jerusalem.

In verse 3, we are told, *"Then Jehoshaphat was afraid and set his face to seek the Lord, and proclaimed a fast throughout all Judah."* This was an impossible situation. On his own, Jehoshaphat had no hope of defeating the armies that were coming against him. But instead of running scared, he ran toward God and prayed.

Jehoshaphat's prayer is one of my favorite prayers from the Bible:

> *For we are powerless against this great horde that is coming against us. We do not know what to do, but our eyes are on you.*   —2 Chronicles 20:12

There have been so many times in my parenting journey when this has been my prayer. I want it to become my kids' prayer, too. Whether it is a relationship struggle, homework situation, grades, friends, or one of the other many challenges our kids may face during the school year, we can't go wrong when we teach them to focus on God first.

Later in chapter 20, we see the people of Judah didn't even have to fight their enemies that day. Instead, God fought the battle for them. All they had to do was collect the spoils.

SOMETHING TO THINK ABOUT

While they are in school, kids need the type of assurance that Judah had. They need to know that they might have struggles, but Jesus goes with them. God is their refuge.

That is where our family's peace is grounded. Not that there won't be conflict, not that they won't struggle with learning or relationships, but we can always be confident that God is with our families.

EXTRA VERSES FOR STUDY OR PRAYER

Second Chronicles 20:1–24, Psalm 29:11, Psalm 46:1–3, John 16:33.

VERSE OF THE DAY

What then shall we say to these things? If God is for us, who can be against us? —Romans 8:31

PRAYER

Lord, may _____ know that You are for them throughout this school year. May Your presence bring them peace.

THINK:

_____

_____

_____

PRAY:

_____

_____

_____

PRAISE:

_____

_____

_____

TO DO:

_____

_____

_____

PRAYER LIST:

_____

_____

_____

QUESTIONS FOR DEEPER REFLECTION

1. What concerns does your family have as we approach this school year? List them below.

_____

_____

_____

2. How does God's promise of His presence bring you peace in the middle of those concerns?

_____

_____

_____

DAY 2

MAY THEY HAVE GODLY FRIENDS

READ ECCLESIASTES 4

Two are better than one, because they have a good reward for their toil. For if they fall, one will lift up his fellow. But woe to him who is alone when he falls and has not another to lift him up! Again, if two lie together, they keep warm, but how can one keep warm alone? And though a man might prevail against one who is alone, two will withstand him—a threefold cord is not quickly broken.
—Ecclesiastes 4:9–12

What is a friend?

I asked my son this question recently. Even though our family has lived in the same house since he was three years old, he has struggled with friendships, and it occurred to me that I didn't know what he thought about the concept of having or being a friend.

Merriam-Webster Dictionary defines a friend as "one attached to another by affection or esteem, one that is not hostile…a favored companion."[2] By this definition, one might have many friends. There are many people for whom I feel affection and even more toward whom I feel no hostility. Since I'm an extrovert, there are also many whom I would call a "favored companion" and enjoy hanging out with.

---

2. *Merriam-Webster*, s.v. "friend," www.merriam-webster.com/dictionary/friend.

Webster even goes on to define "friend" as a verb and includes "friending" on social media. By that definition, our circle of friends might be endless.

As I talked to my son that day, I realized that his definition was quite the opposite of Webster's. Instead of defining "friend" broadly, he had narrowed it down to those who shared his interests and were always nice to him. I realized then that the reason he felt he had no friends all these years wasn't because there were no children available to be friends with, but because whenever someone hurt him, even unintentionally, he struck them off the "friend" list.

That day, we talked about a healthier definition of friends. Yes, friends are often people with whom we have common interests, but even good friends will accidentally hurt us. No, we don't want to be close friends with someone who is repeatedly mean, but our friends will not be perfect.

As I've heard from many sources, one of the biggest influences on our kids' decision to follow Christ long term is their friends. Time and time again when I ask families about the differences in their children as adults, their friends as teenagers are frequently cited as an influence. As author Monica Swanson said in a podcast episode on friendship, "Show me your friends, and I'll show you your future."[3]

That is why helping my son find good friends and have an accurate idea about friendship is so important! I want him to have friendships like the one spoken about in our key verse for today in Ecclesiastes. Those friends can pick him up and help him withstand the struggles that might come his way.

Throughout the Bible, we see evidence of these kinds of friendships. David and Jonathan are a prime example. Throughout David's rise from shepherd to king, Jonathan encourages him and even sometimes saves him from his own father, Saul. During one

---

3. Monica Swanson, "On Friendships, Lonely Seasons, and Making Wise Choices," *The Boy Mom Podcast with Monica Swanson and Friends*, September 12, 2019; monicaswanson.com/episode-19.

particularly trying time in 1 Samuel 23:13–18, Saul is looking everywhere for David to kill him. As Saul gets closer and closer to where David and his men are hiding, Jonathan comes to encourage David and remind him of God's promise that David will be the next king.

Godly friends remind our kids of God's promises when our kids may be tempted to be discouraged and give up. Friends encourage us to keep going when the odds seem against us.

SOMETHING TO THINK ABOUT

We want to encourage our kids to not only seek out these kinds of friends but to be this kind of friend for others. We want them to be in relationships like that in Proverbs 27:17: *"Iron sharpens iron, and one man sharpens another."*

This school year, let's have conversations with our kids about their closest friends. Ask if they are friends who draw them closer to God and encourage them or ones who draw them away.

Let's also encourage our kids to be good, godly friends for others.

EXTRA VERSES FOR STUDY OR PRAYER

First Samuel 23:13–18, Job 4:3–4, Proverbs 27:17, 1 John 3:14–18.

VERSE OF THE DAY

Two are better than one, because they have a good reward for their toil. For if they fall, one will lift up his fellow. But woe to him who is alone when he falls and has not another to lift him up! Again, if two lie together, they keep warm, but how can one keep warm alone? And though a man might prevail against one who is alone, two will withstand him—a threefold cord is not quickly broken. —Ecclesiastes 4:9–12

PRAYER

Lord, may _____ find friends
who will stand by them and support them. May they be this kind of
friend for others.

THINK:

_____
_____
_____

PRAY:

_____
_____
_____

PRAISE:

_____
_____
_____

TO DO: ## PRAYER LIST:

_____   _____
_____   _____
_____   _____

QUESTIONS FOR DEEPER REFLECTION

1. What are the characteristics of a good friend as you would define it?

_____

_____

_____

2. How can you encourage your child to develop those character traits and look for them in others?

_____

_____

_____

DAY 3

MAY THEY HAVE FRIENDS WHO DRAW THEM TO JESUS

READ LUKE 5

And behold, some men were bringing on a bed a man who was paralyzed, and they were seeking to bring him in and lay him before Jesus, but finding no way to bring him in, because of the crowd, they went up on the roof and let him down with his bed through the tiles into the midst before Jesus.
—Luke 5:18–19

There were several times during my college years that I questioned my faith and wondered if God was real.

During an especially hard time when my parents were separated, I wondered, *Why do I hurt so bad if God loves me so much?* Instead of answering that question directly, God spoke to me through my friends.

One Wednesday night after church, my friend Beth stopped me and asked how I was doing. She was one of those friends who saw through my mask right to my heart, so there was no pretending with her. I immediately teared up. We walked to a nearby picnic table and spent the next two hours talking. While I shared my hurt and my heart, she encouraged me and pointed me toward God.

Another time during that same school year, I confessed to my friend Katie that I was questioning God's existence. Knowing I'm a big fan of books and logical explanations, she soon gifted me a copy of *Rock Solid Faith I* by Bert Thompson.[4] Reading that book helped to cement my faith and reassure me of God's existence. Through my friendships with Beth and Katie, I found my way back to God and developed an even stronger faith.

The paralytic in the book of Luke also had these types of friends. When they couldn't reach Jesus through the door of the house, they took their friend to the roof and lowered him down in front of Jesus. I love this story because when the man was weak and unable to come to Jesus himself, his friends carried him, removed the barriers, and laid him down at Jesus's feet.

That is what my friends did for me in college, and what I hope my sons' friends will do for them. My prayer is that they develop friends like those Solomon talks about in the book of Proverbs: *"A friend loves at all times, and a brother is born for a difficult time"* (Proverbs 17:17 csb). Good friends won't run when difficult times come but will bring my kids to Jesus.

SOMETHING TO THINK ABOUT

It isn't always easy to find these types of friends. Sometimes our families are blessed with these types of friendships easily. At other times, we have to go and find them.

The first step is always prayer. It is always to bring our kids to Jesus and ask Him to do what only He can in their lives and their friendships.

As you pray, He might bring to mind families to reach out to, activities to get involved in, or churches to try out. Through the years, God has helped us finally begin to help my son and his brothers find friends in all these ways, but it took courage on my part—courage to

---

4. Bert Thompson, *Rock Solid Faith I: How to Build It* (Montgomery, AL: Apologetics Press, 2000).

reach out, to show up, and to move on when something wasn't bringing about the friendships we had hoped for.

When we begin in prayer and act on what we hear the Spirit saying, we can be confident that God will come through!

EXTRA VERSES FOR STUDY OR PRAYER

Proverbs 17:17, Proverbs 18:24, 1 Thessalonians 4:9.

VERSE OF THE DAY

And behold, some men were bringing on a bed a man who was paralyzed, and they were seeking to bring him in and lay him before Jesus, but finding no way to bring him in, because of the crowd, they went up on the roof and let him down with his bed through the tiles into the midst before Jesus. —Luke 5:18–19

PRAYER

Lord, please send _____ friends who will do whatever it takes to get them to You.

THINK:

_____

_____

_____

PRAY:

_____

_____

_____

PRAISE:

_____

_____

_____

TO DO: PRAYER LIST:

_____   _____

_____   _____

_____   _____

QUESTIONS FOR DEEPER REFLECTION

1. Does your child have this type of friend? If not, where might you begin to connect them with good friends?

_____

_____

2. What are ways you can encourage your child to be this type of friend?

_____

_____

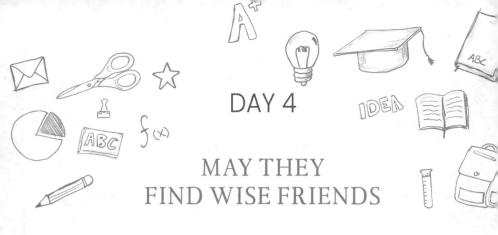

DAY 4

MAY THEY FIND WISE FRIENDS

READ PROVERBS 13

Whoever walks with the wise becomes wise, but the companion of fools will suffer harm.
—Proverbs 13:20

Many times throughout my life, I've asked my friends for advice. All of us rely on our friends at times to help us make a decision. The key is to carefully consider which friends we're asking.

In 1 Kings 12, Rehoboam didn't consider whose counsel he was seeking. He had just become king after his father Solomon died. The people came to him and asked him to lighten their load, and he told them to go away and return in three days.

During those three days, he asked his father's counselors and his own friends for advice. His father's counselors told him to answer the people kindly, so they would always be faithful to him. His friends told him to answer the people harshly and say, *"And now, whereas my father laid on you a heavy yoke, I will add to your yoke. My father disciplined you with whips, but I will discipline you with scorpions"* (1 Kings 12:11).

Instead of listening to the older, wiser advisors of Solomon, Rehoboam chose to follow his friends' advice, and it didn't go well for him. He quickly lost the ten tribes of Israel, retaining only Judah and Benjamin, and the kingdom was never again one complete people.

The advice our kids take sometimes might make little difference in their lives, but at other times, it can profoundly affect our children's future. Having good friends who give wise advice during critical moments is essential in order for our kids to stay strongly connected to God.

+ In elementary school, when they wonder how to treat the new kid, they need friends who encourage them to choose kindness.
+ In middle school, when they wonder if they should cheat on a test, they need friends who encourage them to choose integrity.
+ In high school, when they face difficult dating decisions, they need friends who encourage them to choose purity.
+ In college, when they want to quit, they need friends who encourage them to choose perseverance.

There are many times throughout our children's lives that the choices they make may depend on the friends they have, and we want those friends to be wise ones who look to God for answers.

SOMETHING TO THINK ABOUT

Who are your children's current friends? What voices are speaking into their life when they have a hard decision? Though we wish we could, we can't always be there for our children. They will be faced with decisions where they only have a moment to choose, and during those times, they need to be surrounded by wise friends.

We can't always control who their friends are, but we can take our kids to church, get them involved in activities, and encourage relationships that can have a positive influence on them.

We can also help our kids be wise friends in the lives of others by encouraging their relationship with God.

Most of all, we can pray. Ask God to provide your children with friends who will speak life to them and pray that your children speak life to others.

EXTRA VERSES FOR STUDY OR PRAYER

First Kings 12:1–19, Proverbs 2:20, 1 Corinthians 15:33, Hebrews 10:24.

VERSE OF THE DAY

Whoever walks with the wise becomes wise, but the companion of fools will suffer harm. —Proverbs 13:20

PRAYER

Lord, may _____ walk with wise friends and become wise.

THINK:

_____
_____
_____

PRAY:

_____
_____
_____

PRAISE:

_____
_____
_____

TO DO:

_____
_____
_____

PRAYER LIST:

_____
_____
_____

QUESTIONS FOR DEEPER REFLECTION

1. What kind of friends is your child walking with?

_____

_____

_____

2. How can you pray for those friends and encourage them?

_____

_____

_____

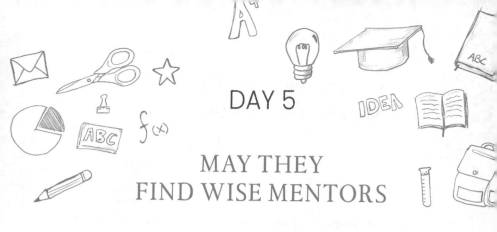

DAY 5

MAY THEY FIND WISE MENTORS

READ PROVERBS 27

Oil and perfume make the heart glad, and the sweetness of a friend comes from his earnest counsel.
—Proverbs 27:9

Shortly after I became a mom, I realized I didn't have a prayer of doing it well on my own. There are simply too many choices and too many "experts" with conflicting advice.

So I looked for moms whose kids were good examples of what I wanted my kids to be like one day. Some of these moms had kids just a few years ahead of mine, while others had grown children, but they all were godly parents whose children were also God followers. Not perfect. Never that. But children who were learning to put God first.

Over and over again during the last twelve years, I've texted these moms for help or sat down at a coffee shop with them to pour out my heart and seek wisdom. During many challenging seasons, they've given me both advice and encouragement to hang in there and keep going.

Like us, our kids need good mentors—not just peers who can offer godly wisdom, but also those who are ahead of them on the journey and can offer sound advice because they've been there.

Even Moses had these types of mentors. In Exodus 18, he is worn out from settling the disputes for all of the people of Israel. I only have three children, and just trying to resolve *their* arguments is exhausting. Can you imagine having to do it for thousands? Moses's father-in-law, Jethro, sees how worn out Moses is. He suggests that Moses appoint wise men to oversee the smaller cases, leaving Moses to handle those that are the most difficult. This plan worked, and Moses was able to get the relief he needed.

Our kids need these types of mentors in their lives. Recently, when I was talking to one of my mentor moms about kid friendships, she said she'd read somewhere that having at least five mentors who aren't their parents greatly raises the chances of our kids staying faithful after they leave home.

These are mentors who they can turn to when they need advice from someone who isn't their parents. As much as I would love to be my children's go-to person for everything, there are times they'll find it easier to talk to someone else, and times when it's easier for someone else to address a heart issue they're struggling with.

Even now, there are times when they have an attitude issue that I cannot nip in the bud. At those times, I've called in other mentors in their lives who they respect to address the struggle. Because they are outside of the situation, sometimes these mentors have a fresh perspective and can help reach our child's heart in a way we can't.

SOMETHING TO THINK ABOUT

There are many places where your child might find these types of mentors. They might be your friends, the parents of their friends, aunts or uncles, ministers at church, coaches, or teachers.

We want to encourage these friendships when we can and be humble enough to step aside and realize this parenting job is bigger than we can do alone. An old proverb says, "It takes a village to raise a child," and helping our kids find wise mentors is the best place to start.

Pray and consider: Who do you already know who might be a good mentor in your child's life? Pray for God to open doors for these types of friendships. He loves to answer these types of prayers!

EXTRA VERSES FOR STUDY OR PRAYER

Exodus 18:13–27, Proverbs 15:23, Proverbs 16:23–24, Romans 12:9–16, Galatians 2:11–21.

VERSE OF THE DAY

Oil and perfume make the heart glad, and the sweetness of a friend comes from his earnest counsel.   —Proverbs 27:9

PRAYER

Lord, bring _____ friends who give godly counsel.

THINK:

_____

_____

_____

PRAY:

_____

_____

_____

PRAISE:

_____

_____

TO DO: ## PRAYER LIST:

_____   _____

_____   _____

_____   _____

QUESTIONS FOR DEEPER REFLECTION

1. Where does godly counsel come from?

_____

_____

_____

2. How can you help your child to become a friend who gives godly counsel?

_____

_____

_____

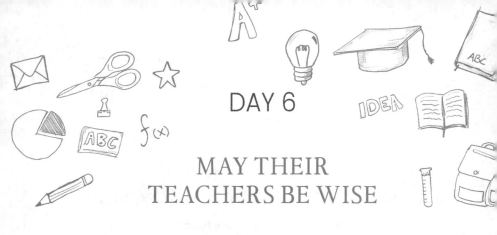

DAY 6

MAY THEIR
TEACHERS BE WISE

READ 1 KINGS 3

*And your servant is in the midst of your people whom you have
chosen, a great people, too many to be numbered or counted for
multitude. Give your servant therefore an
understanding mind to govern your people,
that I may discern between good and evil, for who is able to
govern this your great people?*
—1 Kings 3:8–9

Teaching is a hard job. In recent years, our teachers have had it harder than ever. With the onset of a global pandemic, teaching has been forever changed. For many, distance and online learning are here to stay.

Because of this situation, teachers must not only know how to prepare a lesson and teach it to children who are in the classroom, they also must become skilled in presenting those same lessons in a distance or online environment.

As a college instructor, I pray 1 Kings 3:8–9 every year over myself and my sons' teachers. In our strength, we don't have a prayer of teaching our students well. They come into our classrooms to learn, but they are often carrying buckets of baggage from hurting homes, overwhelming situations, and other struggles. Not only do we need to adapt to different learning struggles, but technology and emotional struggles are also par for the course.

Solomon, too, found himself overwhelmed by what was required of him when he became king of Israel. In our verse today, he's telling God that he's not equipped to lead Israel well and asking, almost begging, for God to grant him the wisdom he needs to do the job. As we know, God answered that prayer abundantly!

God wants to do the same for our children's teachers. Whether your children are homeschooled, online distance learners, or face-to-face in a school environment, your child's teacher needs wisdom from God to do the job well. His Word tells us, *"If any of you lacks wisdom, let him ask God, who gives generously to all without reproach, and it will be given him"* (James 1:5). What an amazing promise!

SOMETHING TO THINK ABOUT

This school year, let's ask God to give our children's teachers wisdom and insight.

We should also be our children's best advocates to help their teachers love and appreciate them. I know one mother of a special needs child who used to write a letter that she entitled "The World According to Zachary" for her son's teachers. We might not have a special needs child, but sending our child's teacher a message that tells them how much we appreciate them and gives them a few insights into how our child learns can be helpful.

This can be especially beneficial if your family is experiencing a struggle that might affect your child's learning. I'm always telling my students, "I want to work with you if you're struggling, but you have to let me know what's going on."

When we join hands with our child's teachers and pray for them, God can *"do far more abundantly than all that we ask or think"* (Ephesians 3:20) by granting the wisdom they need this school year.

EXTRA VERSES FOR STUDY OR PRAYER

First Chronicles 22:12, Proverbs 4:11, Proverbs 16:16, James 1:5–6.

VERSE OF THE DAY

And your servant is in the midst of your people whom you have chosen, a great people, too many to be numbered or counted for multitude. Give your servant therefore an understanding mind to govern your people, that I may discern between good and evil, for who is able to govern this your great people?

—1 Kings 3:8–9

PRAYER

Lord, give all the teachers wisdom and insight this school year. Bless and prosper their efforts.

THINK:

_____

_____

_____

PRAY:

_____

_____

_____

PRAISE:

_____

_____

_____

TO DO:

_____

_____

_____

PRAYER LIST:

_____

_____

_____

QUESTIONS FOR DEEPER REFLECTION

1. What insight do you hope your child's teachers will have into your child this school year?

_____

_____

_____

2. How can you pray for your child's teachers specifically?

_____

_____

_____

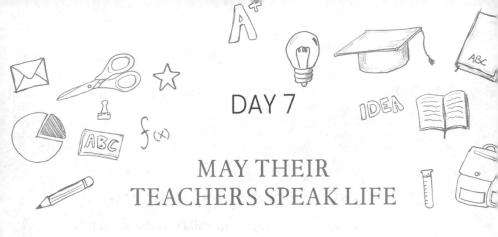

DAY 7

MAY THEIR
TEACHERS SPEAK LIFE

READ 1 THESSALONIANS 5

*Therefore encourage one another and build one another up,
just as you are doing.*
—1 Thessalonians 5:11

Early in the spring, I got "the call" from my son's principal.

Not the kind of call saying someone was unkind to him. Instead, *he* had been mean to someone else and earned a visit to the principal's office.

This time, he was in trouble for something he did, and his discipline was to write a note of apology to the child he had hurt since this was the first offense.

I sat down with the principal and my son to discuss what had happened, not knowing what to expect. Instead of speaking to me, she turned to my son, got down on his level, and began by saying, "Now, I know this isn't the kind of kid you are…"

Over the next few minutes, I watched as she spoke life to his little heart. My eyes teared up, not because he was in trouble. He was—big trouble. But I felt a wave of appreciation and gratitude because even in this situation, the principal encouraged my son and spoke forward into who she knew he could be.

We see Jesus doing this same thing with His disciples. On one occasion, He asks them, *"Who do you say that I am?"* (Matthew 16:15). Peter gives that A-plus student answer: *"You are the Christ, the Son of the living God"* (verse 16). Jesus then changes this disciple's name to Peter and tells him *"on this rock I will build my church"* (verse 18).

At this time, Peter wasn't yet "the rock" he would become or deserving of all Jesus said about him. Just a few verses later, we see Jesus rebuking Peter because he didn't have the things of God in mind.

Many times throughout Jesus's ministry, He speaks life to those around Him. He sees beyond what they have done to who they are capable of becoming, just as my son's principal did that day.

SOMETHING TO THINK ABOUT

I pray my children will have the kind of teachers and principals who speak with kindness. *"Gracious words are like a honeycomb, sweetness to the soul and health to the body"* (Proverbs 16:24). Having teachers who can speak a word of encouragement at just the right time can change a child's course.

Many times throughout my own school life, a teacher's encouragement or discouragement made as much difference on my final class grade as did my ability. I've seen the same thing occur in my children's lives. Several times, they have begun school struggling in a particular subject but the encouragement and support of their teacher turned them around and helped them to grow and improve in that area.

My prayer, for my children and yours, is that they will have teachers who see past shortcomings, mistakes, and test scores to see our children's value and potential and speak life. With these types of teachers, our children will have a better chance at success and grow up to be those who see the best and speak life to others, too.

EXTRA VERSES FOR STUDY OR PRAYER

Proverbs 15:23, Proverbs 16:24, Isaiah 50:4, 1 Thessalonians 5:14.

VERSE OF THE DAY

Therefore encourage one another and build one another up, just as you are doing.   —1 Thessalonians 5:11

PRAYER

Lord, fill all the teachers with life-giving words and build them up so they can pour into our children.

THINK:

_____

_____

_____

PRAY:

_____

_____

_____

PRAISE:

_____

_____

_____

TO DO: PRAYER LIST:

_____   _____

_____   _____

_____   _____

QUESTIONS FOR DEEPER REFLECTION

1. What kind of things show your child love and appreciation? Share those ideas with their teacher.

_____

_____

_____

2. How can you speak life to your child's teacher this school year?

_____

_____

_____

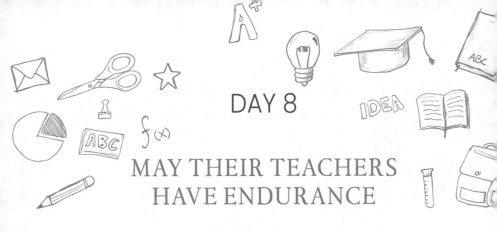

DAY 8

MAY THEIR TEACHERS
HAVE ENDURANCE

READ COLOSSIANS 1

*Being strengthened with all power, according to his glorious
might, for all endurance and patience with joy.*
—Colossians 1:11

As a writing teacher at a hands-on technical school, there are so
many times when I need God's strength. On the first day, my students often tell me that they don't think they need my class. They sit
there, slouched in their chairs with their arms crossed, daring me to
prove them wrong.

Like all teachers, I know what I'm teaching them is important.
They can't go far in life without being able to write and communicate
well, but convincing some of my students of this is another matter.
Even if they do believe in the value of what I'm teaching, so many
outside forces work against them to keep them from succeeding.

To overcome those barriers, I lean into God's wisdom and
strength daily.

Like me, Moses also had to learn to rely on God as he began
to lead the Israelites. When God called him in Exodus chapters 3
and 4, Moses had been hiding in the wilderness from Pharaoh for
forty years, tending his father-in-law's sheep. He was the picture

of someone who had been overwhelmed by his circumstances and wanted to hide.

Even as God called him, Moses gave excuses to explain why he wasn't the man for the job. The people wouldn't listen, he couldn't speak well, God should send someone else... Each time, God assured Moses of His presence and gave him the tools he needed to complete the task.

As we know from the rest of Exodus, Moses did learn to lean into God's strength and trust His leading. Thus he became one of the most influential leaders in Israel's history.

SOMETHING TO THINK ABOUT

God can do the same for our children's teachers, whether that's us or someone else. Teaching can be overwhelming, but when teachers lean into God, He can provide His presence, strength, and the tools needed.

If our children's teachers are not Christians, we can pray for God to lead them to Him. If they are Christians, we can pray He grants them the wisdom to seek Him daily for guidance. Either way, we can pray for God to strengthen them and empower them for the task He's called them to and work with them to help our kids.

EXTRA VERSES FOR STUDY OR PRAYER

Exodus 4:10–12, 1 Corinthians 15:57–58, Galatians 6:9, Ephesians 3:14–16.

VERSE OF THE DAY

Being strengthened with all power, according to his glorious might, for all endurance and patience with joy.

—Colossians 1:11

PRAYER

Lord, grant teachers the strength and endurance they need to do their best as they teach our children.

THINK:

_____

_____

_____

PRAY:

_____

_____

_____

PRAISE:

_____

_____

_____

TO DO: PRAYER LIST:

_____   _____

_____   _____

_____   _____

QUESTIONS FOR DEEPER REFLECTION

1. What are the circumstances your child's teachers find themselves in this school year?

_____

_____

_____

2. How can you encourage them?

_____

_____

_____

DAY 9

MAY GOD GRANT US STRENGTH

READ ISAIAH 41

Fear not, for I am with you; be not dismayed, for I am your God; I will strengthen you, I will help you, I will uphold you with my righteous right hand.
—Isaiah 41:10

After two years of doing karate with my boys, I almost quit.

In January, I went into my belt test anxious and stressed. In the weeks leading up to the test, I worked daily to perfect my punches, kicks, and forms.

As I began the test, I did my best, but the stress made my shoulders tense and my jaw clench.

Then the time came for the board breaks. If you have kids in karate or have ever watched someone break a board, it looks easy. You might have even thought, *Hey, I can do that.* It's not easy, and you probably couldn't do it.

I watched the other adults doing their board breaks, and one after another broke not just one but two boards. One board worried me. Two made me want to sink into the mat.

I approached the boards when it was my turn and took my fighting stance. I pulled my hand back for a palm-heel strike and rammed it forward. Nothing. Not even a crack in the first board. I pulled back my hand again and again. With every hit, pain shot through my wrist, but the board stayed intact. I wondered if my wrist was broken. I wondered, *If everyone else broke two boards, why can't I?*

Finally, my instructor dropped one of the boards on the floor, and I broke the single board with ease. But it didn't matter. I felt like a failure and hung my head as I went to sit back down.

When they called my name for my promotions, I received my next stripe, but that second board taunted me.

Once the test was over, I gathered my things and mumbled a quick goodbye to my friend. I looked longingly at her green belt and felt defeated. That level meant three more boards to break. Three more times to experience pain and possible failure. I wasn't sure I was up to the task.

A few weeks later, after I had had a chance to calm down, I mentioned to one of our instructors that I was afraid I'd broken my wrist during the belt test. She spent that class showing me how to break the board correctly. In karate, they always tell us that our power comes from our hips, but it can be very hard to remember this.

As the instructor had me break board after board, even two boards at once, I learned how to use the strength from my hips, not my arm or leg. And when the next belt test came a few months later, I was ready. This time, I remembered to use my hips. When it came time to break the board, I did so with confidence.

SOMETHING TO THINK ABOUT

In karate, the strength needed to break a board comes from our hips; in life, the strength we need to help our children comes from God. Over and over again, the Bible reminds us of this truth.

The Lord is my strength and my shield; in him my heart trusts, and I am helped; my heart exults, and with my song I give thanks to him. The Lord is the strength of his people; he is the saving refuge of his anointed. —Psalm 28:7–8

When we try to do it on our own, it's a struggle. We often feel frustrated and want to give up right along with our kids! But when we lean into God's strength and ask His Spirit for wisdom, we can gain supernatural insight and strength that we just don't have on our own.

EXTRA VERSES FOR STUDY OR PRAYER

Deuteronomy 31:6–8, Psalm 29:11, Psalm 89:15–18, Ephesians 6:10.

VERSE OF THE DAY

Fear not, for I am with you; be not dismayed, for I am your God; I will strengthen you, I will help you, I will uphold you with my righteous right hand. —Isaiah 41:10

PRAYER

Lord, please strengthen and uphold _____ this school year. May we walk not in fear but in confidence, knowing You are with us.

THINK:

PRAY:

PRAISE:

_____

_____

_____

TO DO:

_____

_____

_____

PRAYER LIST:

_____

_____

_____

QUESTIONS FOR DEEPER REFLECTION

1. Where does your strength come from?

_____

_____

_____

2. How can you look to God as your family deals with new challenges this school year?

_____

_____

_____

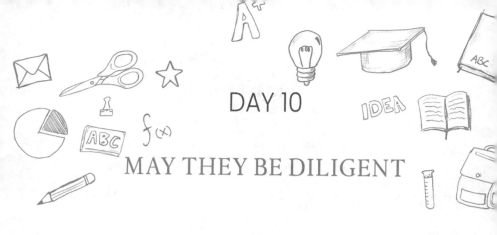

DAY 10

MAY THEY BE DILIGENT

READ PROVERBS 10

A slack hand causes poverty, but the hand of the diligent makes rich. He who gathers in summer is a prudent son, but he who sleeps in harvest is a son who brings shame.
—Proverbs 10:4–5

When I began second grade, I couldn't read well.

It wasn't because my mom hadn't read to me enough when I was little. She had. It wasn't because I wasn't smart enough. I was… though applying myself was another matter. The problem seemed to be that I just didn't learn the way my previous school taught reading. Good ol' *Dick and Jane* books didn't do the job.

That school year, I went to reading lab each week. My reading teacher used fun games, and she was encouraging in all the best ways. Even though I was behind, I don't remember ever being embarrassed or ashamed. I worked hard at learning to read and by the time I entered third grade, I'd caught up with my classmates.

Quickly, reading became a refuge instead of a hindrance. By sixth grade, I was the kid on the playground swing who read while the other kids raced around the schoolyard. Reading allowed me to escape the monotony of school and discover worlds that didn't exist in my little Pennsylvania town. Although I was never a straight-A student, I did become a voracious reader and eventually a teacher.

So when my son struggled with reading in first grade, I was determined to dig in and help him. The whole school year, we practiced and made it fun as we sat for thirty minutes each morning in the car line after dropping off his brother. The car became our classroom and by the end of the school year, he was mostly caught up. We never spent hours drilling on sight words or focusing on what he couldn't do. Instead, he went to the reading specialist, as I did as a kid, and we practiced a little bit each day.

This is the diligence spoken of in Scriptures like Proverbs chapters 6 and 10. It isn't a work ethic that works itself *to the bone*. Instead, it is the tenacity to show up each day and take one step closer to your goal.

We see this kind of diligence in the story of Noah. (See Genesis 6:13–22.) Can you imagine being handed the task of building a boat that was almost one and a half football fields long and over four stories tall, all without modern equipment? If Noah had tried to build it quickly, he would have burnt out. It just wasn't possible. Instead, he diligently worked on it for between fifty and seventy years, a task that took daily persistence.

SOMETHING TO THINK ABOUT

If your child is struggling with being diligent in school—which happens with most children at one time or another, by the way—give them grace.

School is hard. Learning is hard. Some of us struggle more than others, but there is always hope. As we're reminded in 2 Chronicles 15:7, *"But you, take courage! Do not let your hands be weak, for your work shall be rewarded."* My son and I didn't become better readers overnight, but we had teachers and family members who worked with us and encouraged us to keep going.

As you're helping your child work hard this school year, remember that speaking life and encouragement can go a long way. Looking for ways to make a hard subject fun can draw you closer instead of pushing your child away. Teaching your child how to divide a big task into small chunks can make overwhelming jobs seem manageable. Choosing a specific time each day to work on growing in an area of weakness can make a big difference over time. God can do a lot with our little.

Learning to be diligent doesn't come all at once but happens in the daily practice of showing up.

EXTRA VERSES FOR STUDY OR PRAYER

Second Chronicles 15:7, Proverbs 6:6–11, 1 Corinthians 15:58, Galatians 6:9.

VERSE OF THE DAY

A slack hand causes poverty, but the hand of the diligent makes rich. He who gathers in summer is a prudent son, but he who sleeps in harvest is a son who brings shame.

—Proverbs 10:4–5

PRAYER

Lord, may _____ apply themselves this school year and be diligent.

THINK:

_____

_____

_____

PRAY:

_____

_____

_____

PRAISE:

_____

_____

_____

TO DO: PRAYER LIST:

_____   _____

_____   _____

_____   _____

QUESTIONS FOR DEEPER REFLECTION

1. What kind of harvest will your child reap from being diligent?

_____

_____

2. How can you build your child up and encourage them to be diligent this school year?

_____

_____

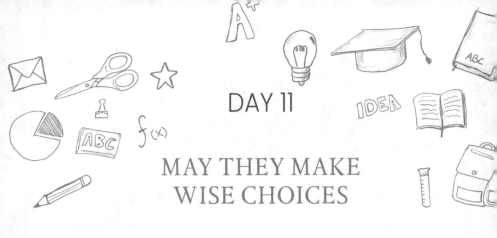

DAY 11

MAY THEY MAKE
WISE CHOICES

READ PROVERBS 2

Yes, if you call out for insight and raise your voice for under-standing, if you seek it like silver and search for it as for hidden treasures, then you will understand the fear of the Lord and find the knowledge of God.
—Proverbs 2:3–5

My dream as a ten-year-old was to be a teacher. Each summer, I created worksheets and set up a classroom in our basement for my younger brother and sister. Many hot summer days were spent in our cool basement as I taught them the math, reading, and writing skills I'd learned the previous school year.

During my master's degree program seventeen years later, the opportunity finally came and I was offered a teaching assistantship. However, saying yes would mean taking a huge cut in pay from my current job at a bank.

My husband and I couldn't agree. For me to have the best chance of teaching college after I graduated, I needed to take the assistant-ship. However, for our family, it would mean pinching pennies a few more years.

I wasn't sure what to do. Over coffee one day, my mentor, Iris, encouraged me to seek God's wisdom in the situation and prayed over me. Her prayer that day was rather unconventional. She knew I was prone to argue—after all, my degree was in composition rhetoric. However, I needed to be willing to listen to my husband that night as we discussed this decision once again.

Instead of praying for wisdom and insight, Iris prayed that God would glue my tongue to the roof of my mouth. Yes, she did!

While hubby and I discussed the situation that night, I wanted to argue and demand my way. I wanted to...but I just couldn't make the words come out. Instead, I listened, rolled over, and went to sleep.

The next morning, my hubby said, "If you want the job, take it." I was shocked. He had never changed his mind like that before. I'm not sure what God did that night, but I am thankful.

Seeking God's wisdom and help in that situation paved the way for me to still be teaching college today.

King David found himself in a similar situation—he needed to listen to God instead of following his desires. He wanted to build the temple for God, but when he sought God about it, God told him no. Instead, He told David that his son, Solomon, would build the temple. So during his lifetime, David made preparations for Solomon. (See 1 Chronicles 22:2–10.) As he passed the baton to Solomon at the end of his life, David even encouraged him to seek God for wisdom and guidance.

SOMETHING TO THINK ABOUT

Our kids will often be put into situations where they are uncertain about which choice to make. They will have to choose between what seems right to them or seek God first for His will on the matter.

It can be tempting to rely on what we think is best, but Job 12:13 reminds us, "*With God are wisdom and might; he has counsel and understanding.*" We need to remind our kids to always seek God and His wisdom first. Our wisdom can often be contrary to God's. I wanted to argue my side on the teaching assistantship; David wanted to build the temple. Neither desire was bad or sinful, but neither was God's will at that moment.

As we encourage our children to seek God first, it is also important to seek wisdom from godly mentors. I would never have thought of a prayer to "glue my tongue" on my own. Iris's years of experience gave her insight that I lacked. God spoke through her to me, and the course of my life was changed.

At school this year, remind your child to seek God's will first and to seek His help in school. Help them to connect to godly mentors who can help them seek God's will when it is hard. They can't go wrong learning to seek God's insight and understanding in the situations they face.

EXTRA VERSES FOR STUDY OR PRAYER

First Chronicles 22:2–13, Job 12:13, Proverbs 23:12.

VERSE OF THE DAY

Yes, if you call out for insight and raise your voice for understanding, if you seek it like silver and search for it as for hidden treasures, then you will understand the fear of the Lord and find the knowledge of God. —Proverbs 2:3–5

PRAYER

Lord, may _____ seek wisdom and understanding. Please give them hearts that want to learn and enable them to understand what they're taught.

THINK:

_____

_____

_____

PRAY:

_____

_____

_____

PRAISE:

_____

_____

_____

TO DO: PRAYER LIST:

_____   _____

_____   _____

_____   _____

QUESTIONS FOR DEEPER REFLECTION

1. From where does your child tend to seek wisdom?

_____

_____

2. How can you encourage them to seek wisdom from God first?

_____

_____

_____

DAY 12

MAY THEY WORK HARD

READ PROVERBS 14

All hard work brings a profit,
but mere talk leads only to poverty.
—Proverbs 14:23 (NIV)

I hated school. From kindergarten through high school, I dreaded school every single morning. I specifically remember being an elementary school student and counting down the years until phonics lessons were done. They were excruciating.

My mom tells me that she spent my first six years of school just trying to get me to sit down, be quiet, and do my homework. She says I would look at an assignment and if I didn't think the effort it took to get an A was worth it, I would choose to get a lower grade. On purpose.

Thankfully, she didn't leave me there and let me give in to my laziness. With persistence—and even some bribery from Grammy for getting A's on my report card—I finally decided to work harder.

Now I get paid to talk in class, and I'm the teacher encouraging my students to hang in there and do the work. My initial struggles make me a better teacher today.

Joseph seemed to struggle as a child, too. Genesis 37 tells us he worked for his brothers as a shepherd, but he also ran to his father and told on them. And dear old Dad, the former Jacob now known as Israel, *"loved Joseph more than any other of his sons, because he was the son of his old age"* (verse 3). Just imagine having a younger sibling who worked for you but was known to be your father's favorite. How would you feel knowing your every action was reported to your father by this son who could do no wrong?

Joseph had a gift with words and dreams, but instead of applying himself, he seemed to use them to stir up trouble and conflict. Shortly thereafter, Joseph was carried off into slavery, but God taught him to use those same gifts to save his family and Egypt.

All of us struggle with our work ethic at some point. Our kids might struggle with one or two subjects or even all of them, like I did. Encouraging them to do the work is not always easy. You may be tempted to hide in the bathroom and scroll through social media instead.

SOMETHING TO THINK ABOUT

On those days when we want to give up the fight and let our kids give in to poor homework or study habits, let's start with prayer. Maybe you need to hide in the bathroom for a minute, but instead of social media, turn to God and ask His Spirit for the strength, wisdom, and insight you need to encourage your child. Pray for God to change your child's heart when it comes to school.

We know that working hard is God's will for our kids. We're told, *"Diligent hands will rule, but laziness ends in forced labor"* (Proverbs 12:24 NIV). We want good lives for our children as adults, and it starts with encouraging a good work ethic when they are young.

As a mom, I pray that the hard work I'm putting in today will pay off tomorrow. *"Let us not become weary in doing good, for at the proper time we will reap a harvest if we do not give up"* (Galatians 6:9 NIV). Mama, your diligence now matters.

Perhaps instead of dreading school, one day, like me, your child will be teaching the class.

EXTRA VERSES FOR STUDY OR PRAYER

Proverbs 12:24, Proverbs 13:4, 1 Thessalonians 4:11–12, 2 Thessalonians 3:10–12.

VERSE OF THE DAY

All hard work brings a profit, but mere talk leads only to poverty.   —Proverbs 14:23 NIV

PRAYER

Lord, may _____ work hard this school year so they may grow and prosper.

THINK:

_____

_____

_____

PRAY:

_____

_____

_____

PRAISE:

_____

_____

_____

TO DO:

_____

_____

_____

PRAYER LIST:

_____

_____

_____

QUESTIONS FOR DEEPER REFLECTION

1. What motivates your child to get tasks done?

_____

_____

_____

2. How can you help encourage your child this school year using that knowledge?

_____

_____

_____

DAY 13

MAY THEY BE STEADFAST

READ JAMES 1

Count it all joy, my brothers, when you meet trials of various kinds, for you know that the testing of your faith produces steadfastness. And let steadfastness have its full effect, that you may be perfect and complete, lacking in nothing.
—James 1:2–4

Without a doubt, the 2020–2021 school year was one of the hardest that children have had to endure—and hopefully, there will never be another year like it again! Whether they were homeschooled or enrolled in private, online, distance, or face-to-face school, the year forced everyone to dig deep to help children continue to learn under challenging circumstances. Even with my online learning and teaching background, my children and I still struggled through online systems that didn't work as planned and keeping up with assignments.

Those times when my youngest son was wrangling with writing and took an hour to write one sentence, I thought, *I teach people eighteen to fifty-five years old how to write all day long. Why can't I teach writing to a first-grader?*

That school year wasn't hard because we didn't have enough patience, our kids didn't want to cooperate, or our school was underprepared. Those things didn't help, certainly, but school was a challenge even under the best of circumstances. And didn't we all survive? We all made it and are stronger for it.

Now, when our families face difficult learning situations in the future, we can look back to 2020–2021 and think, *We survived that, and we can survive this.*

This mindset is exactly what James is talking about in our verses today, and what Paul addresses in his letter to the Romans. He writes:

We rejoice in our sufferings, knowing that suffering produces endurance, and endurance produces character, and character produces hope, and hope does not put us to shame, because God's love has been poured into our hearts through the Holy Spirit who has been given to us. —Romans 5:3–5

When we suffer or are put under pressure, it teaches us endurance. The Greek word for endurance is *hypomonē*, defined as "steadfastness, constancy, endurance," and in the New Testament, it's "the characteristic of a man who is not swerved from his deliberate purpose and his loyalty to the faith and piety by even the greatest trials and sufferings."[5]

This means that suffering helps our families dig in and endure. It helps us stay true to our purpose and follow God, eventually giving us a stronger character and—as that tremendously difficult school year proved—giving us hope for the future.

Interestingly, without stress, we lose the ability to endure. This idea was perhaps best demonstrated by the Biosphere 2 project in Oracle, Arizona. After it began in the 1990s, researchers found that the trees inside grew quickly, but without wind to force them to produce stress wood, they weren't strong enough to support their own weight. Although it seemed like Biosphere 2's massive closed domes would insulate the trees and keep them safe, in the end, it hurt them more than it helped.

---

5. Larry Pierce, *Blue Letter Bible*, s.v. "*hypomonē*," www.blueletterbible.org/lexicon/g5281/kjv/tr/0-1.

SOMETHING TO THINK ABOUT

The same is true for our kids. We would love to insulate them from difficult school years. We want their lives to be free from many of the challenges *we* experienced, but truthfully, stress makes them stronger. When our children's challenges are overcome and we look back on them, we see that they have strengthened their character and given them hope for how God will care for them in the future. This hope and the steadfastness that it produces in them helps our kids to *"be perfect and complete, lacking in nothing"* (James 1:4).

As we go through this school year, instead of avoiding challenges, let's teach our children to embrace them, to seek God's help through them, and allow them to produce hope in God and His work in their lives.

EXTRA VERSES FOR STUDY OR PRAYER

Romans 5:3–5, 2 Corinthians 12:9–10, Colossians 1:11–12, Hebrews 12:1–2.

VERSE OF THE DAY

Count it all joy, my brothers, when you meet trials of various kinds, for you know that the testing of your faith produces stead- fastness. And let steadfastness have its full effect, that you may be perfect and complete, lacking in nothing. —James 1:2–4

PRAYER

May _____ be steadfast this school year and find joy in the work.

THINK:

_____

_____

_____

PRAY:

_____

_____

_____

PRAISE:

_____

_____

_____

TO DO: PRAISE LIST:

_____   _____

_____   _____

_____   _____

QUESTIONS FOR DEEPER REFLECTION

1. In what areas of school does your child struggle with being steadfast?

_____

_____

_____

2. How can you brainstorm ideas together to help them have more endurance in those areas?

_____

_____

_____

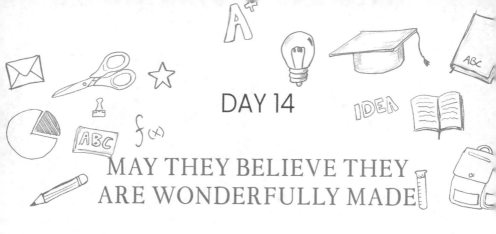

DAY 14

MAY THEY BELIEVE THEY ARE WONDERFULLY MADE

READ PSALM 139

I praise you, for I am fearfully and wonderfully made.
Wonderful are your works; my soul knows it very well.
—Psalm 139:14

During fifth grade, several girls bullied me relentlessly. This was long before bullying was a buzzword. Despite my parents' numerous visits to the school, nothing ever changed.

I dreaded school every single day. One girl loved to hiss at me during music class, "This land is my land, this land's not your land, from California to the New York island…" Another girl in my class would one day invite me into her circle of friends and share her coveted Lisa Frank art case with me—filled with a rainbow of crayons, perfectly sharpened colored pencils, and markers that didn't bleed through the paper—then the next day, she would invite the other girls around her desk, but for no reason I ever learned, she would bar me from the art case. It seemed to be a game with her.

Then there was my classmates' name-calling and the whispered remarks. Though my parents constantly reminded me, "Sticks and stones can break my bones but words can never hurt me," I knew the truth all too well. Words cut deep.

As the year went on, I pulled into myself. No longer was I the bubbly outgoing girl who had entered school that year. Instead, I became withdrawn and kept to myself. I only answered the teacher's questions if I had to and tried to become invisible. I wish I could tell you that one book, a conversation with my mom, a Bible verse, new friends, or a quick fix helped. But they didn't. Instead, it was God slowly wooing me over the next decade through all those things that finally helped me grow into a different, more confident, person.

SOMETHING TO THINK ABOUT

If your child is struggling to believe the truth about who they are, keep praying and keep showing up. The reminders, the verses, the songs, and the seeds you're planting are not wasted. Whether from bullying or another challenge, it takes time to let God's truths sink into our children's hearts.

Reading verses like Psalm 139:14 over and over again until their truth sunk deep into my heart was instrumental in helping me believe God's truth. Despite what those girls in fifth grade said, God said I was *"wonderfully made,"* and He had a plan and purpose for my life. (See Jeremiah 29:11.)

Throughout the Bible, God reminds our children how special they are to Him. In Genesis 1:26–27, they learn they are made in His image; in Psalm 139:14, they discover they are wonderfully made; in Isaiah 62:4, God says He delights in them; and in the Gospels, we see Jesus inviting the children to come to Him because He loves and values them. (See Matthew 18:1–14.)

Keep showing up, Mama. Keep praying. God can do a lot with your little, and He promises that the time in His presence is well spent.

EXTRA VERSES FOR STUDY OR PRAYER

Genesis 1:26–27, Psalm 100:3, Isaiah 64:8, 1 Timothy 4:12.

VERSE OF THE DAY

I praise you, for I am fearfully and wonderfully made. Wonderful are your works; my soul knows it very well. —Psalm 139:14

PRAYER

Lord, we praise You for the special, unique way You designed
_____. May they know how wonderful they are.

THINK:

_____

_____

_____

PRAY:

_____

_____

_____

PRAISE:

_____

_____

_____

TO DO: PRAYER LIST:

_____   _____

_____   _____

_____   _____

QUESTIONS FOR DEEPER REFLECTION

1. What is special and unique about your child?

_____

_____

_____

2. How can you remind them of those qualities this school year?

_____

_____

_____

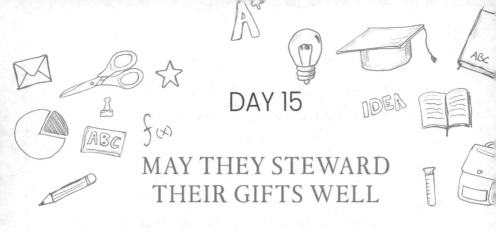

DAY 15

MAY THEY STEWARD THEIR GIFTS WELL

READ EPHESIANS 2

For we are his workmanship, created in Christ Jesus for good
works, which God prepared beforehand,
that we should walk in them.
—Ephesians 2:10

I would like to take credit for the strawberries growing prolifically in my backyard, but I can't. I'm truly the laziest gardener ever; their growth is all God's doing. A few years ago, I set the pot of strawberries my mom gave me on the ground, and they have taken off, placing runners and now covering a large area.

This year, as I checked my strawberry plants expecting sweet red berries, all I found were red berries on top and rot underneath. All of them. We didn't get a single berry worth eating.

To harvest fruit worth eating, I'll have to steward my plants better next year.

The same is true for our children. I see gifts in each of my sons that did not come from me. They're good gifts planted by God. Left to their own devices, my sons may choose to use their good gifts to be selfish and hurt others. Most kids do. However, if I can help them steward those gifts well, they will more than likely end up being a blessing.

My youngest son loves to entertain. He craves a crowd. As we go through our days, his big personality can be a challenge, but it can also be a blessing. A few years ago, he became good buddies with a lady at church. She always told him how much she loved to see him sing with the kids on stage during services. Under her praise, his eyes just sparkled.

When she found out she had cancer and had to travel for her treatments, he started to ask me to send videos of him singing to her. He would make up a song and dance on the spot and have me record it. For many months until God called her home, my son brightened her chemo treatment days with his songs. He still struggles to channel his big personality well, but I point us both back to how he was such a blessing to my friend, to remind us of the good that can come from it.

SOMETHING TO THINK ABOUT

In the Gospels, we see that Peter has a big personality. He frequently speaks up without thinking and is corrected for it. However, in Acts, God uses that big personality to spread the gospel throughout Israel and the surrounding region, and Peter rises as a leader in the early church. God can take the gifts He's given us, like those He gave Peter, and teach our children to use those gifts to serve and bring glory to God.

God also made our children special in unique ways. Maybe they are good at math, drawing, reading, kindness, building, music, sports...the list is endless. As parents, we have the opportunity to help them channel those gifts for good and God's glory.

EXTRA VERSES FOR STUDY OR PRAYER

Psalm 138:8, Matthew 25:14–30, Philippians 1:6, Colossians 1:10.

VERSE OF THE DAY

For we are his workmanship, created in Christ Jesus for good works, which God prepared beforehand, that we should walk in them. —Ephesians 2:10

PRAYER

Lord, may _____ know that they are Your workmanship and discover the good works You have planned for them.

THINK:

_____

_____

_____

PRAY:

_____

_____

_____

PRAISE:

_____

_____

_____

TO DO:

_____

_____

_____

PRAYER LIST:

_____

_____

QUESTIONS FOR DEEPER REFLECTION

1. How can you already see God's hand on your child in the special ways He made them?

_____

_____

_____

2. How can you help them steward those gifts well?

_____

_____

_____

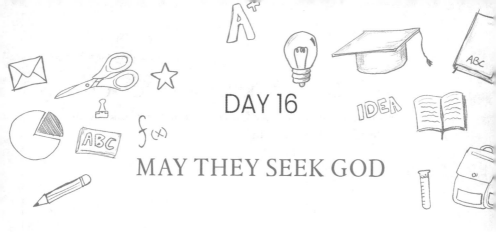

DAY 16

MAY THEY SEEK GOD

READ PSALM 37

*The steps of a man are established by the Lord, when he
delights in his way; though he fall, he shall not be cast headlong,
for the Lord upholds his hand.*
—Psalm 37:23–24

Since college, I have been a project junkie. Whether participating in a club, volunteer work, teaching, writing, or sports, I am the person who is running around trying to keep multiple plates spinning while praying they don't come tumbling down on my head.

Over the years, I have experienced burnout several times, but as soon as I had any energy, I jumped back into the spinning plate act. The activities were always "good" things—clubs that connected people, volunteer programs that saved children, writing that encouraged, teaching that pointed to Jesus, and sports that connected with other believers. They weren't bad activities.

Then in the fall of 2020, the exhaustion hit harder than it ever had before. For months, I was so tired, I could hardly see straight. Many nights, I would fall into bed at 7 p.m. like I did when I was pregnant, but I knew that wasn't a possibility. After a year of doctor's visits and blood tests, I was diagnosed with chronic fatigue syndrome. For several months, I threw a mental hissy fit. Imagine a three-year-old kicking and screaming at the zoo, and you've got the picture. Ever so slowly, God began peeling activities and responsibilities out of my hands. I felt like Gideon and his shrinking army. (See Judges 7.) I kept asking, "Is this enough?" And God would shake His head and gently say, "No, not yet. Keep letting go."

Over those months, God began whispering to my heart that His will for me wasn't more activities. It was more of Him.

Unsurprisingly, David in Psalm 37 shares a similar message. Over and over, we're reminded, *"Commit your way to the Lord"* (verse 5), and *"Be still before the Lord and wait patiently for him"* (verse 7). The theme of this psalm is that even when the wicked and those around us seem to be succeeding and passing us by, we need to put our trust in God, seek Him, and wait for Him.

As I've learned to wait, He's taught me to:

+ Focus on Him first and leave the growth to Him
+ Ask Him about my next steps before jumping headlong
+ Go deep in a few things instead of being shallow in many

These lessons have been so hard for me to learn. They are hard for our kids to learn, too.

SOMETHING TO THINK ABOUT

Our kids are often encouraged to be better, faster, and stronger, to do more. It is often framed in the context of making it into the best school and getting scholarships for college. These seem to be worthy goals—and they are. Like all my activities over the last twenty years, those aren't bad things.

But as Psalm 37 tries to teach us, our kids need to bring those plans before God. They need to ask Him what activities He wants them to commit to during this season.

Instead of being spread thin over many good things, maybe we need to go deep into just one or two.

Instead of more activities that lead to burnout over and over again, maybe they just need more of Him.

EXTRA VERSES FOR STUDY OR PRAYER

Psalm 121:3–8, Proverbs 3:21–23, Proverbs 16:9.

VERSE OF THE DAY

The steps of a man are established by the Lord, when he delights in his way; though he fall, he shall not be cast headlong, for the Lord upholds his hand. —Psalm 37:23–24

PRAYER

Lord, please establish _____ steps and uphold them as they follow You.

THINK:

_____

_____

_____

PRAY:

_____

_____

PRAISE:

_____

_____

_____

TO DO:

_____

_____

_____

PRAYER LIST:

_____

_____

_____

QUESTIONS FOR DEEPER REFLECTION

1. What plans is your child making right now for school or other projects?

_____

_____

_____

2. How can you encourage them to bring those things to God and ask Him for wisdom and guidance?

_____

_____

_____

DAY 17

MAY THEY BEAR FRUIT

READ PSALM 1

But his delight is in the law of the Lord, and on his law he meditates day and night. He is like a tree planted by streams of water that yields its fruit in its season, and its leaf does not wither. In all that he does, he prospers.
—Psalm 1:2–3

I have three very loud, very energetic boys. As Brooke McGlothlin says, "They are 250 percent boy!"

Despite my best efforts, they continue to wrestle like puppies when it's not appropriate, hurt each other with their words, and use force when words would do. I have reminded them over and over again—or as my middle son recently told me, "A hundred million times!"—"You take care of *you*." Whoever does this will help his brothers act better, too.

Over the years, I have also invited my sons into Jesus's presence and planted seeds of prayer, Bible reading, devotionals, nightly blessings, and memorizing verses. Not perfectly, not even daily, but I aim to teach them that walking with Jesus is a daily relationship, not a list of rules.

Now and then, I get a glimpse of the fruit of those seeds when one of them helps his brother without being asked, shares unexpectedly, and speaks words of encouragement.

This is what David is talking about in Psalm 1. As we plant the seed and invite our children to take roots in God's water, they begin to bear fruit in their season.

That last bit is the very hardest for me as their mama.

I want to see that fruit *now*, or even yesterday.

This process can be slow and difficult. I wish it worked as fast as the weeds that sprout up in my garden overnight. Instead, David accurately compares the way of the righteous to a fruit tree. The apple tree in our backyard is just now bearing fruit—six years after we planted it. And it just has a few apples.

SOMETHING TO THINK ABOUT

With our tree and with my children, it can be tempting to become impatient, to demand fruit now after all the care and attention. But frustration will not do any good and won't help them produce fruit.

Only by our faithfully continuing to plant and water those seeds in our children will they eventually produce fruit. During hard times, I hold onto the promise in Galatians 6:9: *"And let us not grow weary of doing good, for in due season we will reap, if we do not give up."*

Our job is to lead them to Jesus, invite them into His presence, and help them grow closer to Him. He will grow the fruit in our children in their season. He will draw their hearts to Him.

EXTRA VERSES FOR STUDY OR PRAYER

Jeremiah 17:7–8, John 15:4–8, Galatians 5:22–24, Galatians 6:9.

VERSE OF THE DAY

But his delight is in the law of the Lord, and on his law he meditates day and night. He is like a tree planted by streams of water that yields its fruit in its season, and its leaf does not wither. In all that he does, he prospers.   —Psalm 1:2–3

PRAYER

Lord, may _____ delight in You and bear fruit in their season.

THINK:

_____

_____

_____

PRAY:

_____

_____

_____

PRAISE:

_____

_____

_____

TO DO:

_____

_____

_____

PRAYER LIST:

_____

_____

_____

QUESTIONS FOR DEEPER REFLECTION

1. What are some of the fruits you see God growing in your child's life?

_____

_____

_____

2. Take time to thank Him for that fruit today.

_____

_____

_____

DAY 18

MAY THEY REMEMBER GOD'S TRUTH

READ MATTHEW 10

Are not two sparrows sold for a penny? Yet not one of them will fall to the ground outside your Father's care. And even the very hairs of your head are all numbered. So don't be afraid; you are worth more than many sparrows.
—Matthew 10:29–31 (NIV)

My son stood in the middle of the karate ring facing a giant. His opponent was easily half a foot taller than him and several years older. As they took a fighting stance to begin sparring, I saw the determination on my son's face. But he lost. Over and over, he lost. He could have blamed it on the fact that the other kids were older and taller, but in reality, he simply wasn't prepared to fight kids so much bigger than him.

By the end of the match, his heart was crushed. I saw his face fall as they announced the winner and presented him with a sword.

Despite his disappointment, or maybe because of it, I have a favorite karate picture of my son that doesn't show him with the winning trophy. Instead, it shows his shoulders hunched and his eyes facing away as one of our karate instructors kneels by his side with his hand on my son's shoulder. You can tell from the photo that the instructor is speaking life and hope to my son's disappointed heart.

The prophet Jeremiah experienced this type of disappointment, too. There were several times throughout his lifetime that instead of viewing him as the hero, the people sought to kill him. (See Jeremiah 26.) However, early on in Jeremiah's ministry, and several times throughout it, God reminds him of who he is. He proclaims His truth over Jeremiah and his ministry: *"I chose you before I formed you in the womb; I set you apart before you were born"* (Jeremiah 1:5 CSB). Knowing God's truth helped to reorient Jeremiah and keep him faithful.

SOMETHING TO THINK ABOUT

This is what our children need to remember every day but especially on hard days. Though we want to see them always get the A and win the contest, they won't.

Their foundation must be something stable that never changes—Jesus. But how do we help our kids get that foundation and build their self-worth on it?

It starts by building during the good times through prayer, reading God's Word, and memorizing what God says about them.

I like to think of memorizing Scripture as a sparring practice against life's adversities. In Ephesians 6:17, we learn that *"the sword of the Spirit...is the word of God."* It is our only defensive weapon against Satan's lies. When we help our kids memorize Scriptures that affirm where their value is found, teach them what that means, and pray it over them, it helps them learn how to wield the sword of the Spirit and arms them for battle in those hard days.

If you need help, you might start with the extra verses listed for study or prayer. During mealtimes, I like to invite my sons to repeat the verse that hangs by our kitchen table. They don't always want to say it, so I don't pressure them, but most of the time they do. The promised ice cream after they've said it ten times helps, too.

I hope that when I tuck God's truth deep in their hearts, it will become the soundtrack of their lives. When hard times come and Satan pours his lies over them, my prayer is that God's truth, the sword of the Spirit, will defend them and speak life to their hurting hearts.

EXTRA VERSES FOR STUDY OR PRAYER

Romans 8:31–39, Ephesians 1:4–5, 1 John 4:9–10.

VERSE OF THE DAY

Are not two sparrows sold for a penny? Yet not one of them will fall to the ground outside your Father's care. And even the very hairs of your head are all numbered. So don't be afraid; you are worth more than many sparrows. —Matthew 10:29–31 NIV

PRAYER

Lord, may _____ know that they are valued by You because they are Yours, not because of their accomplishments.

THINK:

_____

_____

_____

PRAY:

_____

_____

_____

PRAISE:

_____

_____

_____

TO DO:

_____

_____

_____

PRAYER LIST:

_____

_____

_____

QUESTIONS FOR DEEPER REFLECTION

1. In what ways does your child struggle with their self-worth?

_____

_____

_____

2. Use the verses in the "Extra Verses for Study or Prayer" section and others to help your child fight Satan's lies with God's truth about them.

_____

_____

_____

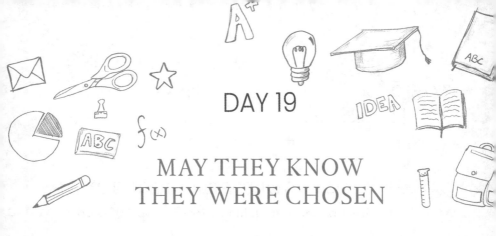

DAY 19

MAY THEY KNOW
THEY WERE CHOSEN

READ 1 PETER 2

*But you are a chosen race, a royal priesthood, a holy nation, a
people for his own possession, that you may
proclaim the excellencies of him who called you
out of darkness into his marvelous light.*
—1 Peter 2:9

My three sons have completely different personalities. From the
time they were born, each has had specific ways they were wired by
God that were obviously unique and unlike their brothers. My oldest
son has loved music since before he was born. Even in my tummy,
he would react to the music we played, and that love has continued.
My middle son loves people. He's always telling me he is friends with
half the school—and I believe him. To be around him is to feel seen
and loved. My youngest son is an entertainer. Whether it is singing,
dancing, or talking, he brings the party wherever he goes.

As I watch them, I feel like Mary, who *"stored all these things in
her heart"* (Luke 2:51 NLT). I see how God made them for a purpose,
and I pray, watch, and wait to see how He's going to develop these
gifts in them, how He's going to use these things for His purpose to
bring glory to Himself through them.

Waiting can be hard. However, I'm confident because I know that God can bring good and glory from everything that happens to them.

We see this idea in the story of Joseph. In Genesis 45, Joseph tells his brothers to not be upset about how they treated him in the past because God was able to use it to save their family. Even in the hard times, Joseph realized he was chosen by God and used the gifts he'd been given as a child, gifts of insight and interpretation of dreams, to bring glory to the Lord.

The trick is teaching our children that they were made for a purpose, and they need to use their gifts to serve others. Or as Peter writes:

> Each of you should use whatever gift you have received to serve others, as faithful stewards of God's grace in its various forms.
> —1 Peter 4:10 NIV

We see Joseph make this transition. In the earlier chapters of Genesis, he shares his dreams and insights, but they aren't well received by his family. Even his father rebukes him in Genesis 37:10, which indicates that Joseph may not have been sharing these gifts in the best tone of voice with the best heart behind them. Sound familiar?

Over the years, Joseph changes. He first uses those same gifts to help the king of Egypt's cupbearer and warn the baker in Genesis 40. Then in Genesis 41, God allows him to use that gift to save a nation.

Joseph's story gives me hope for my kids. Right now, they often use their gifts to irritate the living daylights out of their brothers instead of using them for good and God's glory.

SOMETHING TO THINK ABOUT

As I pray for wisdom, God can help me teach my sons how to steward these gifts well. He can open doors for my boys to use them for His good, just as he did for Joseph. He can reveal His purpose for them. He can, as Brooke McGlothlin taught me to pray years ago, turn hearts of stone into hearts of flesh. (See Ezekiel 36:26.)

My daily prayer for them is that they would know they were chosen by God for God to bring glory to God.

EXTRA VERSES FOR STUDY OR PRAYER

Genesis 45:1–8, Isaiah 43:18–21, Matthew 5:14–16, 1 Peter 4:10–11.

VERSE OF THE DAY

But you are a chosen race, a royal priesthood, a holy nation, a people for his own possession, that you may proclaim the excellencies of him who called you out of darkness into his marvelous light.   —1 Peter 2:9

PRAYER

Lord, may _____ know they are chosen by You and use their gifts to glorify You.

THINK:

_____

_____

_____

PRAY:

_____

_____

_____

PRAISE:

_____

_____

_____

TO DO: PRAYER LIST:

_____   _____

_____   _____

_____   _____

QUESTIONS FOR DEEPER REFLECTION

1. How can your child point others to God even now?

_____

_____

_____

2. How can you lead by example by giving glory to God with your own gifts?

_____

_____

_____

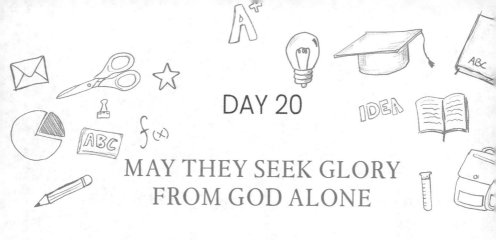

DAY 20

MAY THEY SEEK GLORY
FROM GOD ALONE

READ JOHN 12

*For they loved the glory that comes from man more than
the glory that comes from God.*
—John 12:43

Some of my favorite things in the world are sunrises and seashells. They constantly remind me that God performs for an audience of one. He doesn't need our praise or glory. They remind me, as I wrote in my last book, that:

> God creates beautiful sunsets on hundreds of thousands of planets every single day that no one sees. It seems like a lot of beauty gone to waste, but I've noticed as I've observed this world God often saves his most beautiful art for secret places—the center of a flower, the inside of a seashell, a mountain top. He's not concerned about anyone's applause, and it makes me think, maybe I shouldn't be either.[6]

Whatever God has asked us to do, He's already done. In Matthew 6:1–4, He tells us to do our good works in secret. Then, along with the creation we see around us, He also gives us the example of Jesus.

---

6. Tara L. Cole, *Abide: 40 Ways to Focus on Jesus Daily* (La Vergne, TN: Lightning Source Inc., 2019), 48.

While in Jerusalem for a holy day, Jesus and His disciples see a paralytic at the pool of Bethesda. (See John 5:1–9.) Season 2 of *The Chosen* offers a powerful vision of how that man could have watched life pass him by as friends and family grew up and moved on with their lives, while he was left crippled.[7] You can see the anguish on his face as dozens of people enter the pool to receive their healing, giving a clear picture of the despair he must have felt by the time Jesus arrives.

But after Jesus heals the man and gives him the hope for which he has waited a lifetime, Jesus doesn't seek any glory. He doesn't even tell the man His name. Later, Jesus asks the Jews at the temple, *"How can you believe, when you receive glory from one another and do not seek the glory that comes from the only God?"* (John 5:44).

SOMETHING TO THINK ABOUT

Thinking this way can be so hard when we, and especially our kids, want the glory. Kids want to show off, receive lots of "likes" on social media, and have people praise them. But Jesus shows us a better way, and creation itself illustrates this better way over and over again.

We can point our children to the stories of Jesus and creation as examples of how God often saves His best work for the hidden places. He gives the example of doing our best, even and especially if He's the only one who will ever see it. (See Matthew 6:1–4.) We can encourage them—and ourselves—that the hidden work we do with intention is not hidden from God. He sees, and He smiles.

EXTRA VERSES FOR STUDY OR PRAYER

Matthew 6:1–4, John 5:1–3, John 5:41–44, 1 Thessalonians 2:1–6.

---

7. *The Chosen*, "The Perfect Opportunity," season 2, episode 4. Directed by Dallas Jenkins. Written by Ryan Swanson, Dallas Jenkins, and Tyler Thompson. TBN, May 11, 2021.

VERSE OF THE DAY

For they loved the glory that comes from man more than the glory that comes from God. —John 12:43

PRAYER

Lord, may _____ seek glory from You this year and not from those around them.

THINK:

_____

_____

_____

PRAY:

_____

_____

_____

PRAISE:

_____

_____

_____

TO DO: PRAYER LIST:

_____   _____

_____   _____

_____   _____

QUESTIONS FOR DEEPER REFLECTION

1. In what ways is your child influenced by the opinions of others?

_____

_____

_____

2. How can you encourage them to seek God's praise?

_____

_____

_____

DAY 21

MAY THEY LOVE OTHERS

READ EPHESIANS 3

That according to the riches of his glory he may grant you to be strengthened with power through his Spirit in your inner being, so that Christ may dwell in your hearts through faith—that you, being rooted and grounded in love, may have strength to com- prehend with all the saints what is the breadth and length and height and depth, and to know the love of Christ that surpasses knowledge, that you may be filled with all the fullness of God.
—Ephesians 3:16–19

I love you even on hard days," I told my son as I hugged him. That day had been particularly challenging, with fits of anger and back talking. I said it as much to remind myself as to remind him. Then, a few weeks later, as I was having a hard day and trying to keep myself in check, he piped up from the back seat of the car, "Mom, I love you even on hard days!"

Isn't that what we all need? To know that no matter what happens, someone loves us and won't give up, even when we're at our worst?

Jesus, too, knew and gave this kind of love. Of course, He didn't have hard days because He Himself misbehaved, but He still had hard days, especially in the week leading to the cross. Recounting the Last Supper, John writes:

Now before the Feast of the Passover, when Jesus knew that his hour had come to depart out of this world to the Father, having

*loved his own who were in the world, he **loved them to the end**.*
During supper, when the devil had already put it into the heart of
*Judas Iscariot, Simon's son, to betray him, Jesus, **knowing that***
the Father had given all things into his hands, and that he
***had come from God and was going back to God**, rose from*
supper. He laid aside his outer garments, and taking a towel,
tied it around his waist. Then he poured water into a basin and
began to wash the disciples' feet and to wipe them with the towel
that was wrapped around him.   —John 13:1–5

Even as the night He's betrayed begins and Judas the betrayer is
present, Jesus demonstrates His love for His disciples. He loves them
fully. I've often thought that this was simply because He was Jesus,
the Son of God, and that's true. However, in verse 3, John points out
that Jesus knew the source of His authority and strength, knew who
He was and where He was going. It was on the basis of this knowledge that He began His final act of service leading to the cross. It
wasn't just *who* He was; it was what He knew to be true.

SOMETHING TO THINK ABOUT

Our kids need this same kind of confidence as they go into the
world and choose to love on hard days. They will struggle to love
others well until they know how much they are loved. It is no accident
that *hurt people hurt people* and *loved people love people*.

As Paul points out, when we are *"strengthened with power through
his Spirit"* (Ephesians 3:16), we can *"know the love of Christ that surpasses knowledge [and] be filled with all the fullness of God"* (verse 19).

We can help our kids to know this kind of love from us and from
God. On hard days, we can reassure them. Let's be honest—our love
for them runs deep. Through our words, tone, and facial expressions,
we demonstrate our love.

We can reassure them of the love of God by pointing them to
Him and His love for them. We can encourage them to turn to God
and ask for His Spirit's strength on hard days. We can pray for God
to show Himself to them and help them comprehend His love.

Once they are assured that they are loved, they will be better prepared to face hard days. Yes, we want to always protect them, but when we do, we rob them of opportunities to learn how to handle difficult situations in a way that honors God.

No, their days won't all be easy, even though we wish they could be. But as we give them a solid foundation built on the love of God, they will be better prepared to weather the hard days and in turn extend that love to others.

EXTRA VERSES FOR STUDY OR PRAYER

Psalm 57:10, Isaiah 43:4, John 13:1–5, Romans 5:5, Colossians 3:14.

VERSE OF THE DAY

That according to the riches of his glory he may grant you to be strengthened with power through his Spirit in your inner being, so that Christ may dwell in your hearts through faith—that you, being rooted and grounded in love, may have strength to comprehend with all the saints what is the breadth and length and height and depth, and to know the love of Christ that surpasses knowledge, that you may be filled with all the fullness of God.
—Ephesians 3:16–19

PRAYER

May _____ be rooted and grounded in the love of Christ and filled with the fullness of God.

THINK:

_____

_____

_____

PRAY:

_____

_____

_____

PRAISE:

_____

_____

_____

TO DO: PRAYER LIST:

_____   _____

_____   _____

_____   _____

QUESTIONS FOR DEEPER REFLECTION

1. What makes your child feel loved?

_____

_____

_____

2. How can you intentionally show love to them on hard days?

_____

_____

_____

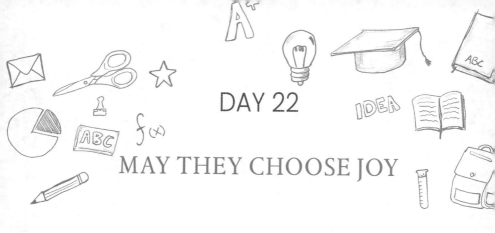

DAY 22

MAY THEY CHOOSE JOY

READ PSALM 126

*Then our mouth was filled with laughter, and our tongue with
shouts of joy; then they said among the nations,
"The Lord has done great things for them."*
—Psalm 126:2

When churches were closed during the COVID-19 pandemic, our family watched a lot of Christian artists' YouTube videos as part of our Sunday morning service time. My youngest son's favorite song to watch was "Joy" by For King and Country. The music video begins with one TV news anchor warning of an impending storm, while another tries to interrupt with some good news. The lyrics talk about how negative messages tend to bring us down and turn our hearts to stone, while the chorus notes that despite the hard circumstances, we can always choose joy.

As one anchor sings, "Though I walk through the valley in the shadow of night, oh with You by my side, I'm stepping into the light." Throughout the rest of the video, one by one, everyone in the TV studio begins to choose joy, and the move of God becomes contagious.[8]

Just like this song suggests, during times of heartache and fear, we all have the opportunity to choose joy. In Nehemiah 8, after Ezra has read the Pentateuch to the Israelites, they weep and repent

---

8. For King and Country, "Joy," on *Burn the Ships* (Word Entertainment, 2018); www.youtube.com/watch?v=lA7n7TwPDmw.

because they realize they have neglected God's law for generations. But Nehemiah tells them, *"Do not be grieved, for the joy of the Lord is your strength"* (Nehemiah 8:10).

We don't think of joy and sadness coexisting. Instead, we consider them to be opposites, thinking that where one is, the other cannot be. But that isn't what the Bible teaches.

Instead, it teaches that our joy is based on God and His unchanging nature. Joy is based on remembering what He has done in the past and trusting Him with our future. In Isaiah 12:2–4, we read:

"Behold, God is my salvation; I will trust, and will not be afraid; for the Lord God is my **strength** *and my song, and he has become my salvation." With* **joy** *you will draw water from the wells of salvation. And you will say in that day: "Give thanks to the Lord, call upon his name, make known* **his deeds** *among the peoples, proclaim that his name is exalted."*

Nehemiah and Isaiah both make it clear that our strength comes from the joy we find in God. That joy isn't based on what is swirling around us or our families, but on remembering and praising God for what He has done in the past. This gives us hope for the future, even when today looks impossible.

SOMETHING TO THINK ABOUT

Even as our kids go to school, this joy can be theirs.

There are several ways we can help them remember what God has done for them. When my kids were little, we played the "Blessing Game" and would see who could think of the most blessings from God during the day. As they've gotten older, we have a "blessing book" lying on our kitchen table. About once a week or so, I'll ask them what blessings they've seen, and I write them down.

I also keep a journal of "God stories" for our family. When God shows up in a big or small way, I write it down so we have a record of it. Writing might not be your family's *thing*, but scrapbooks, picture boxes, drawing, and painting are all different ways your family can remember what God has done to help you draw your strength and joy from that hope instead of the circumstances around you.

EXTRA VERSES FOR STUDY OR PRAYER

Nehemiah 8:10, Psalm 28:7–8, Psalm 92:4, John 15:11.

VERSE OF THE DAY

Then our mouth was filled with laughter, and our tongue with shouts of joy; then they said among the nations, "The Lord has done great things for them." —Psalm 126:2

PRAYER

May_____ remember what God has done for them and find joy in the work of His hands.

THINK:

_____

_____

_____

PRAY:

_____

_____

_____

PRAISE:

_____

_____

_____

TO DO:

_____

_____

_____

PRAYER LIST:

_____

_____

_____

QUESTIONS FOR DEEPER REFLECTION

1. What blessings have you seen in your life in the last twenty-four hours?

_____

_____

_____

2. How can you encourage your children to find joy and hope by remembering what God has done for them?

_____

_____

_____

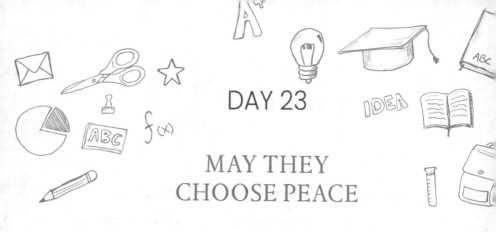

DAY 23

MAY THEY
CHOOSE PEACE

READ ISAIAH 26

*You keep him in perfect peace whose mind is stayed on you,
because he trusts in you.*
—Isaiah 26:3

Peace is a choice.

My grandmother recently told me that when my uncle was young, he got into an argument with the boy next door. It was enough of a conflict that the other mother got involved, and she was pretty upset.

The next day, Grammy collected some fruit she had just bought and knocked on the neighbor's door. She didn't mention the conflict; she just held out the fruit and said, "I just thought your son might enjoy some bananas." The other mother looked shocked and accepted the fruit.

After that, she would wave when she saw Grammy, and their families got along.

Learning to get along with others is a choice.

Our karate instructor once told my boys, "There is no conflict until there is a reaction." My grandmother could have reacted poorly that day and let a children's conflict become an adult conflict. She had the choice to take up my uncle's side and *go set the record straight*, but she chose peace instead.

Jesus frequently chose peace instead of violence. In John 10, he is in Jerusalem and the people have asked him to tell them straight out if he is the Messiah or not. He instead refers to the work He's done in *"my Father's name"* (John 10:25). The people are enraged and get ready to stone Him. Instead of defending Himself, Jesus asks them more questions and eventually walks away. He could have defended Himself physically. He could have justified himself verbally. Instead, He asks questions and again refers them to the work He's doing.

Our kids have many opportunities to choose peace, too. So often, the conflicts they find themselves in with their siblings, friends, or classmates could have been stopped if one of the parties chose to react differently by choosing peace.

SOMETHING TO THINK ABOUT

Choosing peace is not easy.

In Psalm 29:11, we learn that peace is a blessing from God. Then in Ephesians 2, we learn that Jesus *"is our peace"* (verse 14) and has reconciled us to God. (See verse 16.) Our kids trust Jesus and accept God's gift of peace once when they become Christians, but then they have the daily choice to accept His gift of peace.

Daily peace is harder. It means trusting God and being kind, even if they want vengeance. It means trusting God and doing the right thing, even if that choice isn't popular. Sometimes it means trusting God and walking away, even when they want to defend themselves.

As always it starts with prayer. Choosing a peaceful path doesn't come naturally. It isn't easy without the supernatural strength of God's Spirit working in our children's hearts and lives.

But with God's help, peace is possible.

EXTRA VERSES FOR STUDY OR PRAYER

Psalm 29:11, John 14:27, Ephesians 2:12–18, Colossians 3:15.

VERSE OF THE DAY

You keep him in perfect peace whose mind is stayed on you, because he trusts in you. —Isaiah 26:3

PRAYER

May _____ trust God and choose peace.

THINK:

_____
_____
_____

PRAY:

_____
_____
_____

PRAISE:

_____
_____
_____

TO DO: PRAYER LIST:

_____   _____
_____   _____
_____   _____

QUESTIONS FOR DEEPER REFLECTION

1. Who do your kids struggle to make peace with?

_____

_____

_____

2. How can you help them to trust God and choose peace even when it is hard?

_____

_____

_____

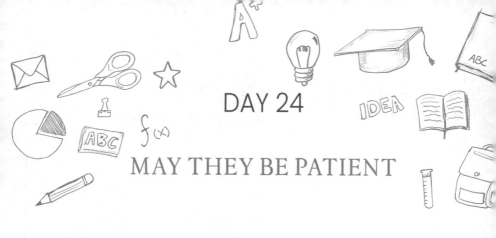

DAY 24

MAY THEY BE PATIENT

READ COLOSSIANS 1

Being strengthened with all power, according to his glorious might, for all endurance and patience with joy.
—Colossians 1:11

Riding in a car with three boys is no joke.

Before we even left the driveway, I heard:

"Mom, he's lying on me!"

"Mom, he hit me!"

"Stop getting in my space!"

"Move your elbow!"

I pulled the car over less than a mile later and warned them sternly that we were not doing all this arguing and fighting today. I told them they needed to stop the arguing, or instead of going to the movies, we would go home, and they could put that energy to good use by cleaning something.

I love these boys, but they try my patience in all kinds of ways. Daily, I need to have patience with them and not lose my temper when they are fighting, complaining, and bickering. I need patience for the long haul as I wait for all the seeds I've planted in their hearts to grow.

But only God can grow those seeds of patience in my heart and theirs.

As we seek to help our kids grow the fruit of the Spirit in their lives, we need to remember it is just that—the fruit of the Spirit, not the fruit of my children or myself.

We haven't a chance of growing this fruit without His help.

Paul's prayers in his letters to the churches are some of my favorites in the Bible. If you want some ready-made prayers for your kids, simply begin reading through Ephesians, Philippians, and Colossians.

In Colossians 1:11, Paul prays that the church at Colossae will be *"strengthened with all power, according to his glorious might, for all endurance and patience with joy."* He reminds the church at Ephesus that the power to do those things comes from the Spirit. (See Ephesians 3:16–19.)

How do we and our children access this power to have daily patience with those around us and enduring patience as we wait for growth? Prayer. In both of those chapters, Paul is praying for his readers. He doesn't tell them to pull themselves up by their bootstraps, try harder, and come up with better ideas. Instead, he prays for God to empower them to do what they cannot.

SOMETHING TO THINK ABOUT

As our kids go to school, let's continue to remember the power of prayer. Yes, they need more patience with others. Yes, they need to be patient and wait when they want something *now*. However, let's begin with prayer and lead them to pray for God to empower them with the patience they need for each new day.

EXTRA VERSES FOR STUDY OR PRAYER

Romans 12:12, Galatians 5:22, Ephesians 4:1–3, James 1:2–5.

VERSE OF THE DAY

Being strengthened with all power, according to his glorious might, for all endurance and patience with joy.

—Colossians 1:11

PRAYER

May _____ be strengthened by God's Spirit to endure and have patience with joy.

THINK:

_____

_____

_____

PRAY:

_____

_____

_____

PRAISE:

_____

_____

_____

TO DO:

_____

_____

_____

PRAYER LIST:

_____

_____

_____

QUESTIONS FOR DEEPER REFLECTION

1. When does your child struggle the most with patience?

_____

_____

_____

2. How can you specifically pray for them to have patience in that situation?

_____

_____

_____

DAY 25

MAY THEY SHOW KINDNESS

READ 2 SAMUEL 9

And David said, "Is there still anyone left of the house of Saul,
that I may show him kindness for Jonathan's sake?"
—2 Samuel 9:1

More than any other time of year, summer is a struggle in kindness. All. Day. Long.

My kids fuss and fight with each other over toys, games, TV shows, food, meaningless objects—you name it. I'm sure your kids do, too.

Because of this struggle, I started a kindness jar a few years ago. The first one we did was an experiment. I had my kids list actions their siblings could do to show kindness to them. The lists were honestly pretty mean, with things like "rub my stinky feet" (I do have boys after all) and similar ideas. Then I informed them that these were the things they would do for their brothers when they needed to practice kindness. Much groaning ensued! That idea worked for a while.

Last year, we did it again, but this time, we listed things that seemed kind to them. The list included doing their sibling's laundry, playing fifteen minutes of video games together, playing outside together, making up a song, and saying three nice things. I tried my best to encourage actions that aligned with each child's love language.

Now, when they are unkind to each other, they draw two ideas from the kindness jar and pick one of them to do. This idea works surprisingly well! Usually, it buys me at least a few hours of peace as the act of being kind helps to mend the hearts of both the one who was wronged and the wrongdoer.

When I remember to use the kindness jar instead of telling them five hundred times, "Stop picking on your brother," our house is more peaceful.

We learn the same idea throughout Scripture. Kindness is contagious and has the power to mend hearts. In 2 Samuel 9, David is seeking someone from Saul's lineage to whom he can show kindness. He discovers Jonathan's son Mephibosheth and invites him to eat at David's table.

Mephibosheth had every reason to expect retribution for all of the pain Saul had caused David, but instead, David gave him back Saul's land and servants. This kindness heals the wounds between the two families.

SOMETHING TO THINK ABOUT

Our children can emulate such acts of kindness. As they learn to practice kindness, even when it is hard, they will find that kindness is contagious. When someone expects hurt but receives kindness instead, it begins to plant seeds of kindness in their own hearts. Yes, sometimes those seeds grow slowly, but we can be confident that they *will* grow.

As we send them off to school each morning, let's encourage kindness.

EXTRA VERSES FOR STUDY OR PRAYER

Proverbs 12:25–26, Ephesians 2:7, Ephesians 4:32.

VERSE OF THE DAY

*And David said, "Is there still anyone left of the house of Saul,
that I may show him kindness for Jonathan's sake?"*

—2 Samuel 9:1

PRAYER

May _____ seek to show kindness to others.

THINK:

_____

_____

_____

PRAY:

_____

_____

_____

PRAISE:

_____

_____

_____

TO DO:

_____

_____

_____

PRAYER LIST:

_____

_____

_____

QUESTIONS FOR DEEPER REFLECTION

1. In what circumstances does your child find it most difficult to show kindness?

   _____

   _____

   _____

2. How can you help them to begin to practice kindness in those situations?

   _____

   _____

   _____

DAY 26

MAY THEY GROW
IN GOODNESS

READ LUKE 6

The good person out of the good treasure of his heart produces good, and the evil person out of his evil treasure produces evil, for out of the abundance of the heart his mouth speaks.
—Luke 6:45

Goodness and kindness are two sides of the same coin.

To help me see the difference, I think of kindness as actions taken while goodness starts internally. Even those we know who aren't Christian are capable of kindness. Anyone can say a kind word, help someone with a task, or give to someone in need.

On the other hand, goodness is not just actions but a state of the heart. Luke 6 provides us with verses that show the difference between these two concepts. Before Luke gets to our key verse for today, he shows what goodness looks like.

First, it is demonstrated in the actions of Jesus as He heals those who come to Him. Then Jesus gives practical application, saying, *"Love your enemies, do good to those who hate you, bless those who curse you, pray for those who abuse you"* (Luke 6:27–28). What follows is a list of actions—turning the other cheek, lending without expecting anything in return, and giving to everyone who needs it. These ideas were revolutionary then, and they still are today.

True goodness goes against the grain. It is a way of acting contrary to what culture tells us is right or fair.

I love that Jesus doesn't simply say, "Do all these things," and leave it at that because the list in Luke 6 is almost as hard as the laws of the Old Testament.

SOMETHING TO THINK ABOUT

So, how do we teach our children to grow in goodness? Jesus says it comes from the good stored in our hearts. To use an analogy, to get cookies out of my oven when my kids come home from school, I first have to put cookies in. To share the goodness of our hearts, we must first store goodness inside.

J. L. Gerhardt writes in *Think Good*, "If you want the Spirit to give you good thoughts, give him something to work with."[9]

We have to help our kids fill up their hearts with goodness so that they can share it. This takes a commitment of years. For our family, it looks like praying together, listening to Christian music, consistent Bible study, memorizing verses, and choosing good movies, books, video games, and TV shows. I try to fill up my children's minds with good things so that as they get older, goodness is the soundtrack in the background of their life.

As you seek to fill your kids up with goodness, start small. Choose just one of the ideas above and start today. God can do a lot with your little.

EXTRA VERSES FOR STUDY OR PRAYER

First Chronicles 16:34, Psalm 100:5, Luke 6:45, Romans 12:21.

VERSE OF THE DAY

The good person out of the good treasure of his heart produces good, and the evil person out of his evil treasure produces evil, for out of the abundance of the heart his mouth speaks. —Luke 6:45

---

9. J. L. Gerhardt, *Think Good: How to Get Rid of Anxiety, Guilt, Despair & the Like to Finally Find Peace of Mind* (Scotts Valley, CA: Createspace, 2016), 58.

PRAYER

May _____ store up good treasure in their heart and produce good fruit.

THINK:

_____

_____

_____

PRAY:

_____

_____

_____

PRAISE:

_____

_____

_____

TO DO:

_____

_____

_____

PRAYER LIST:

_____

_____

_____

QUESTIONS FOR DEEPER REFLECTION

1. In what area does your child have the greatest struggle with goodness?

_____

_____

_____

2. How can you begin to fill up your child's heart with good things, so good will come out?

_____

_____

_____

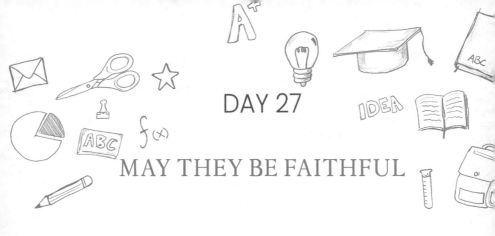

DAY 27

MAY THEY BE FAITHFUL

READ PSALM 26

For your steadfast love is before my eyes,
and I walk in your faithfulness.
—Psalm 26:3

As much as I love taking karate with my boys, there are many days when I want to quit. I grow weary of picking them up after school and listening to them whine about going straight to practice. I get tired of keeping track of uniforms and weapons. Goodness, some days *I* don't even want to show up for practice.

But I remain faithful to the commitment we made.

If I quit, my kids would probably quit too, and that wouldn't be good. I know the friends and community found at Christian Karate Academy are needed during this season of life for me and my sons. The discipline, commitment, and practice learned through karate provide a good foundation for the rest of their lives. Just the energy they get to release in constructive ways is advantageous!

Sometimes faithfulness can be hard to understand. The Hebrew word for "faithfulness" in the Psalms is *'emuwnah* and it means "firmness, fidelity, steadfastness, steadiness."[10] It means that even when something is hard, even when we don't want to, we do not waver. We stay the course.

---

10. *Bible Study Tools*, s.v. "'emuwnah," www.biblestudytools.com/lexicons/hebrew/kjv/emuwnah.html.

Don't get me wrong. Every activity we join isn't meant to be a long-term commitment. My boys did T-ball for a few years, but when they wanted to try karate the next season, we said okay.

Teaching our kids to stick to commitments they have made and stay faithful is a valuable lesson. It is a good foundation for learning to stay faithful to God.

Over and over again in the Old Testament, we're told of God's steadfast love and faithfulness. We see these aspects of the Lord demonstrated in the Old Testament, but they really come alive in Jesus. Jesus is a tangible reminder of God's faithfulness to His promise to David.

Despite hundreds of years of unfaithfulness on the part of Israel, God remained faithful, kept giving them second chances, and finally fulfilled His promise to give David a descendant who would reign forever.

It is God's faithfulness that prompts our own.

SOMETHING TO THINK ABOUT

Staying faithful to God and His ways can be so hard for our kids, especially in the face of everything that goes on at school and online.

For years, this Scripture has given me hope: *"If we are faithless, he remains faithful—for he cannot deny himself"* (2 Timothy 2:13). It reminds me that even when I mess up, even when my kids mess up, Jesus is still there, remaining faithful. *"Jesus Christ is the same yesterday and today and forever"* (Hebrews 13:8).

As your kids struggle with faithfulness this school year, continue to remind them of God's faithfulness. No matter what, He's always there with open arms, inviting them into His presence and His story. Pray for them to be captivated by His steadfast love and faithfulness, even as they practice being faithful themselves.

EXTRA VERSES FOR STUDY OR PRAYER

Psalm 100:5, Psalm 119:30, Psalm 119:90, 2 Timothy 2:13.

VERSE OF THE DAY

For your steadfast love is before my eyes, and I walk in your faithfulness. —Psalm 26:3

PRAYER

May _____ be captivated by God's steadfast love and walk in faithfulness.

THINK:

_____

_____

_____

PRAY:

_____

_____

_____

PRAISE:

_____

_____

_____

TO DO: PRAYER LIST:

_____   _____

_____   _____

_____   _____

QUESTIONS FOR DEEPER REFLECTION

1. When does your child experience the greatest struggle with faithfulness?

_____

_____

_____

2. How can you encourage them to be faithful even when it is hard?

_____

_____

_____

DAY 28

MAY THEY BE GENTLE

READ PHILIPPIANS 4

Let your gentleness be evident to all. The Lord is near.
—Philippians 4:5 (NIV)

Gentleness is one of the hardest ideas to teach my children because they often confuse it with weakness.

However, when I think of gentleness, I picture the large, rough hands of a farmer holding a new baby chick. Those hands are strong. They have thrown hay bales, fixed tractors, and worked cattle, but when they hold that baby chick, they are gentle. Their strength is controlled.

Jesus gives us the best example of this type of strength being under control, being gentle. The night Jesus is crucified, Peter denies Him. Three times, Peter tells others that he does not know the Lord, despite telling Jesus hours earlier that he would remain faithful no matter what. (See Luke 22:31–62.)

After His resurrection, when Jesus sees Peter again, He could have berated His disciple or cast him aside for his failure to remain faithful. Instead, Jesus restores Peter gently.

Jesus takes Peter off by himself and three times asks him, *"Do you love me?"* And Peter answers, *"You know that I love you."* Then Jesus tells him, *"Feed my lambs...Tend my sheep... Feed my sheep"* (John 21:15–17). These three times correspond to the three times Peter denied Jesus. Three times, Jesus gave Peter the chance to affirm his love and commitment to Him.

SOMETHING TO THINK ABOUT

As we seek to be gentle with our children and teach them what gentleness looks like, all of us can learn from Jesus's example.

Gentleness isn't being weak or letting others walk all over us. Instead, it is remaining faithful to God and His standards of love and kindness. It's shown in the tone of voice and touch used to correct a child. It is shown in extending hot chocolate and a listening ear to a struggling teen instead of harsh discipline.

In our children, we see it as they stoop down to help another kid who has fallen, lay a hand on a hurting friend's shoulder, or give a hug. We see it as they walk away from a fight and ignore hurtful words instead of getting revenge. Gentleness is not easy. Daily, our kids will need to call on the Holy Spirit to help them be gentle when they face difficult situations. Some days it may still feel like weakness.

However, when we set our eyes on Jesus, we learn that gentleness is anything but weakness. It is controlled strength.

EXTRA VERSES FOR STUDY OR PRAYER

Proverbs 15:4, Matthew 11:29, Ephesians 4:1–3.

VERSE OF THE DAY

Let your gentleness be evident to all. The Lord is near.
—Philippians 4:5 NIV

PRAYER

May the gentleness of _____ be evident to all who see them.

THINK:

_____

_____

_____

PRAY:

_____

_____

_____

PRAISE:

_____

_____

_____

TO DO: PRAYER LIST:

_____   _____

_____   _____

_____   _____

QUESTIONS FOR DEEPER REFLECTION

1. When is it most difficult for your child to be gentle?

_____

_____

_____

2. How can you point them to the example of Jesus to help them learn that gentleness is not weakness but strength controlled?

_____

_____

_____

DAY 29

MAY THEY
SHOW SELF-CONTROL

READ TITUS 2

*For the grace of God has appeared, bringing salvation for all
people, training us to renounce ungodliness and worldly passions,
and to live self-controlled, upright, and godly lives in the present
age, waiting for our blessed hope, the appearing of the glory of
our great God and Savior Jesus Christ, who gave himself for
us to redeem us from all lawlessness and to purify for himself a
people for his own possession who are zealous for good works.*
—Titus 2:11–14

I stood in front of my bedroom mirror and cringed as I stared at my new haircut. Rather than featuring the wavy layers of Rachel from *Friends*, I looked like a poodle, with short layers that poofed out every which way. I dreaded walking into my ninth grade class the next day. I imagined the gawks and giggles from the other girls whose hair looked like they could be on the cover of *Glamour* magazine.

I grabbed the ends of my hair and wrenched the hairbrush through the mess, trying to make the layers softer or less voluminous, but they only grew. I looked like a poodle who'd stuck its paw in a light socket.

In frustration, I chucked my hairbrush across the room and heard it snap. As I picked up the pieces of my favorite brush, tears filled my eyes. Now I not only had a Halloween worthy haircut, but I had no way to tame it.

This was just one of many times when my anger quickly boiled to the surface, causing me to say or do things I regretted later. Growing up, I struggled a lot with self-control.

All the fruits of the Spirit are hard without the Spirit's help, but love and self-control bookend the list for a reason. (See Galatians 5:22–23.)

As 1 Corinthians 13 tells us, without love, the other fruits mean nothing, but as we grow in the others, we are growing in self-control. All of the others boil down to laying aside ourselves for someone else, learning to let go of selfishness, and concerning ourselves with the interests of others. (See Philippians 2:3–4.)

One of my friends put it this way: "Self-control is wielding and yielding our power well."

We see this type of self-control from Jesus in the garden of Gethsemane. After Judas comes and kisses Jesus, Peter takes his sword and cuts off the ear of a servant of the high priest who has come to arrest Jesus. Instead of taking up the fight, Jesus immediately rebukes Peter, saying:

> *Put your sword back into its place...Do you think that I cannot appeal to my Father, and he will at once send me more than twelve legions of angels? But how then should the Scriptures be fulfilled, that it must be so?*   —Matthew 26:52–54

Then Jesus reaches out and heals the servant's ear. (See Luke 22:51.)

Hearing the words *"twelve legions of angels"* might not mean much to us today, but that's 72,000 angels! They could have easily set Jesus free and even overcome the Roman Empire, as the Jews hoped He would. But instead, Christ is self-controlled. He yields His power and lays aside His feelings to lay down His life so that we can be saved.

SOMETHING TO THINK ABOUT

I wish I could tell you that as you teach your children self-control, they will learn it overnight. I wish I could tell you that you will see instant answers as you pray the prayers in this journal. You might... but again, you might not.

What I do know is that as we point our kids to Jesus—the One who is for them, made them with a purpose, and grows them through His Spirit—we will begin to see the fruit of that labor over years and decades.

Self-control is one of the most visible fruits of the Spirit, but it begins to be seen as the others are grown. Unlike my strawberries that produced fruit the first year, self-control is like my apple tree, taking years of care and unseen growth before offering up a harvest. It is a slow process.

Keep pressing on, dear Mama. As we pray, *"in due season we will reap, if we do not give up"* (Galatians 6:9).

EXTRA VERSES FOR STUDY OR PRAYER

Proverbs 25:28, 2 Timothy 1:7, 2 Peter 1:5–8.

VERSE OF THE DAY

For the grace of God has appeared, bringing salvation for all people, training us to renounce ungodliness and worldly passions, and to live self-controlled, upright, and godly lives in the present age, waiting for our blessed hope, the appearing of the glory of our great God and Savior Jesus Christ, who gave himself for us to redeem us from all lawlessness and to purify for himself a people for his own possession who are zealous for good works.

—Titus 2:11–14

PRAYER

May _____ turn away from ungodliness and live a self-controlled and godly life, as they wait in hope for Jesus's return.

THINK:

_____

_____

_____

PRAY:

_____

_____

_____

PRAISE:

_____

_____

_____

TO DO: PRAYER LIST:

_____   _____

_____   _____

_____   _____

QUESTIONS FOR DEEPER REFLECTION

1. When does your child struggle most with self-control?

_____

_____

_____

2. How can you begin to help them develop more self-control in that area?

_____

_____

_____

DAY 30

MAY THEY TRUST GOD

READ PROVERBS 3

Trust in the Lord with all your heart, and do not lean on your own understanding. In all your ways acknowledge him, and he will make straight your paths.
—Proverbs 3:5–6

Do you trust me?

That seems to be a question asked throughout the Bible. From beginning to end, people's actions are based on how they respond to it.

When the serpent tells Eve, *"You will not surely die"* (Genesis 3:4), he contradicts what God told her. By taking the apple, Eve demonstrates that she believes what the serpent told her over what God had said.

We see the same response from the Israelites throughout their forty years of wandering in the wilderness. Over and over again, they complain to Moses because they don't trust God to care for them and do what He promised.

God asks our children the same question: "Do you trust Me?"

Our prayer is that they ultimately trust Him for their salvation, but even after they become Christians, they have the daily choice to trust God.

When they are underprepared for a test or an assignment, do they trust God or cheat?

When their friends are teasing the outcast, do they join in or stand up for the other kid?

When their friends are all going to a party where they know there will be drugs and alcohol, do they go or pass?

When they procrastinate on a responsibility, do they own up or lie?

It can be hard for our children to make the right choices and trust God when they feel like they are standing alone and the circumstances look impossible. David, too, had this choice when he had to deal with King Saul, whose jealousy made him try to kill David for many years.

In 1 Samuel 26:7–11, David hears that Saul is camped nearby and sneaks into Saul's camp at night. The warrior who accompanies David asks him for permission to kill Saul, but David refuses. Instead, he trusts God to fulfill His promise to give the kingdom to David in God's time.

Can you imagine the inner struggle David must have fought? Saul had murdered the priests who helped David, he gave David's wife to another man, and he pursued David all over the wilderness when David had only brought blessings to Saul. Yet David held back. He made the hard choice, the unpopular choice, and trusted God.

SOMETHING TO THINK ABOUT

Our kids will face hard choices throughout their lives. As young children, the choices have lesser consequences, but the ramifications of their actions grow as they get older. Some choices to trust God over what they feel and see may affect them for a lifetime.

While they are with us, we have the opportunity to first show what it looks like to trust God in our own lives and then help them do the same. When we face hard choices, we can verbalize our thought process for our kids and demonstrate what it looks like to choose to trust our Lord. They will face many hard choices as they grow up, and we can come alongside them and invite them to believe in God's promises and plans for them.

It can be so easy for our kids to trust in what they can see, such as their own skills, friends, and peers. But we can point them toward God and with David, we can say, *"We trust in the name of the Lord our God"* (Psalm 20:7).

EXTRA VERSES FOR STUDY OR PRAYER

First Samuel 26:12, Psalm 20:7, Isaiah 30:15–16.

VERSE OF THE DAY

Trust in the Lord with all your heart, and do not lean on your own understanding. In all your ways acknowledge him, and he will make straight your paths. —Proverbs 3:5–6

PRAYER

May _____ trust in the Lord and follow His path for them.

THINK:

_____

_____

_____

PRAY:

_____

_____

_____

PRAISE:

_____

_____

_____

TO DO:

_____

_____

_____

PRAYER LIST:

_____

_____

_____

QUESTIONS FOR DEEPER REFLECTION

1. In what areas does your child find it hardest to trust God?

_____

_____

_____

2. How can you encourage them to give those areas of their life to God and trust Him even then?

_____

_____

_____

ABOUT THE AUTHOR

Tara L. Cole is a teacher, wife, and mother to three active boys. She earned a B.A. in English from Freed-Hardeman University and a master's degree in Composition and Rhetoric from the University of Central Oklahoma.

Tara has taught communications and writing courses since 2007 at various universities in Oklahoma, both in person and online. She is currently a communication faculty member at Oklahoma State University Institute of Technology.

Tara is a recipient of the 2019 Award for Teaching Excellence from the National Institute for Staff & Organizational Development and the 2020 Regents Distinguished Teaching Award.

Along with teaching, Tara's passion is helping moms and their kids deepen their relationships with Jesus. Her previous book, *Abide: 40 Ways to Focus on Jesus Daily*, and her podcast Over A Cup help women connect with Jesus throughout their day.

Learn more at taralcole.com.